unraveling motherhood

Understanding Your Experience

Through Self-Reflection,

Self-Care & Authenticity

Geraldine Walsh

FOREWORD BY DR. MALIE COYNE

Hatherleigh Press is committed to preserving and protecting the natural resources of the earth. Environmentally responsible and sustainable practices are embraced within the company's mission statement.

Visit us at www.hatherleighpress.com and register online for free offers, discounts, special events, and more.

Unraveling Motherhood

Library of Congress Cataloging-in-Publication Data is available upon request.

ISBN: 978-157826-964-8

Printed in the United States

10 9 8 7 6 5 4 3 2 1

Disclaimer: This book is designed to help us unravel certain aspects of our lives which can become knotted as we birth not only our offspring but also ourselves. This period of transition is heavily based within our minds and as a result our mental wellbeing. This book is not intended as a replacement for the professional advice a therapist can provide you. If you are concerned regarding your thoughts, behaviors, or actions, please seek professional support, advice, and care.

To my girls, Allegra and Devin,

for making me a mother and encouraging this unraveling.

And to my Barry.

Contents

This Is Me

This is me.
Not just Momma.
Not defined by motherhood
Or landed in a colorless empty box
Of womanhood.

This is me.
The dreamer, the writer, the poet,
The artist, the creator, the thinker,
The coffee addict, the energetic mother,
The happy daughter,
The content and modern woman.

The beginning of a story,
The tense middle,
But nowhere near the end.

—Geraldine Walsh

Foreword
by Dr. Malie Coyne

WHEN ASKED TO WRITE this foreword, I jumped at the chance to lend support to Geraldine's 'unraveling' of motherhood, as it is in the sharing of her own personal struggles, blended with her vast experience of mental wellbeing, that I have felt freer to share my own struggles. The hope is that you will, too. After all, we are all imperfect mamas, and I truly believe that being messy together is better. Sure, we've still got a lot of learning to do, but look how much we've learnt already!

In the words of Geraldine, *"For too long, we have swept the tough parts of motherhood under the rug in the hope that no one notices the difficult truth that motherhood is not perfect."* By continuing to do this as a society, who are we serving, exactly? We're not helping ourselves as mothers who continually feel like we're not up to scratch for this emotional rollercoaster of a job. Nor are we serving our children, as an overwhelmed parent is a less self-reflective parent with reduced abilities to look after our own needs and the emotional needs of our children.

In our modern society, where there is huge pressure to perform to our best in every aspect of our lives, there is an erroneous belief that we can somehow "master" motherhood in the same way that we tackle everything else. Add to this, new mothers are bombarded with information on the "do's and don'ts" of being a good parent from family, friends, experts, and the perception that everyone else is doing it "perfectly" on social media. This is a pressure cooker to someone who is totally sleep-deprived and feels very vulnerable looking after a baby for the first time or navigating motherhood's intense ups and downs, with often little acknowledgement or support.

The belief that a "perfect mother" exists promotes feelings of inadequacy, loneliness, and blame. Feeling like we don't quite measure up begins a spiraling of negative thoughts, which leads to low self-confidence and emotional difficulties. We need to continue to shatter falsehoods that there is such a thing as a "perfect mother" by calling it out for what it is. This is exactly what Geraldine does in the pages that follow, as she unravels this erroneous belief and encourages us to attune to our inner selves and, *"Find our own truth, identity, and purpose to live a profound and fulfilled life during the many intensely exhausting and overwhelming periods of motherhood".*

In my 20 years of practice as a clinical psychologist with children and families, I have often referred to the importance of being a 'good enough' parent. The "good-enough parent" is a concept derived from British paediatrician and psychoanalyst Winnicott in the 1950s in his efforts to provide support for what he called "the sound instincts of parents...stable and healthy families." Fast-forward 70 years, this concept is as relevant as ever, with what I often refer to as the '3 pillars of good parenting', including 1) learning to trust your gut instinct; 2) letting go of the fallacy of perfection; and 3) getting to know yourself as a parent and prioritizing self-care. These concepts ring through loud and clear in this book, which is a testament to Geraldine's belief that we already have what we need to be good parents and that "unraveling" our stories can only enhance our precious offerings.

Apart from her openness with struggling with the transition to motherhood and her own personal experience of anxiety and depression, Geraldine's entire freelancing career has revolved around researching and writing content on mental health, family, health, and women's issues, which she always delivers with heart and true authenticity. What's more, this book is backed up by insightful contributions from highly skilled professionals, including unraveling identity with Dr. Janina Scarlet, unraveling triggers with Allison Keating, unraveling flaws with Dr. Mary O'Kane, unraveling control with Aisling Leonard-Curtin, and unraveling boundaries with Dr. Lisa Coyne.

I have read lots of parenting books, but what I most appreciate about this one is that I'm not left feeling deflated and inadequate, reaching for a giant bar of chocolate. I am by no means a 'perfect mother' and having included my own personal struggles in my recent book, fellow parents told me they most benefitted from a "tell it like it is" approach rather than one which offered a wagging finger, "this is how you should parent" approach. Truth be told, there are no "should's" with parenting. We do our best, sometimes we mess up, and we always keep trying.

As I embarked on writing this foreword after a fairly relaxed summer's day, one of my girls had a screaming fit when I commented on her behavior and told her, "Your sister is going to get an extra YouTube clip the next time." As we were driving through her screams, I was reminded (yet again!) of the chaos of motherhood and how a lovely moment can suddenly turn into what seems like the worst moment. The "AND" aspect of parenting is something Geraldine balances impeccably: *"Recognizing the shortcomings [of parenting] does not make us ungrateful for what we have... Know that changing your outlook, searching for yourself, sometimes resenting the 'job' and having strong emotions and thoughts is freeing. You can be grateful AND look for change and growth"*.

Not only does Geraldine unravel many aspects of motherhood, but she also skillfully stitches things up without pretending that all will be perfect: *"There is no perfection in any of this unraveling"*. This book is a wonderful toolkit to work through those confusing internal thoughts throughout motherhood. It offers evidence-based, tried, and tested self-care tools and techniques to guide us through the noise, including mothering ourselves, enhancing self-acceptance, self-compassion, and self-care, recognizing mind traps, and building psychological flexibility. The clarity of this book means that you can read it cover to cover or delve into it chapter by chapter in your own time.

If you know anything about my work, you will know that I am all about the power of self-compassion, which taps into our body's self-healing system, reduces fear and anxiety, and increases our ability to soothe ourselves and our children during challenging times. Self-care isn't just something we do to escape life's pressures. It's about refilling your cup and creating that crucial space between stimulus and response, so we can make calm and sometimes difficult decisions to create a life we don't need to regularly check out of. Geraldine unravels the knots many of us hold around self-compassion (why is it so hard?), so we can recognize our common humanity as imperfect mamas, accept our feelings for what they are without judgement, and show kindness to ourselves when we struggle. Better yet, her simple methods for practicing self-compassion are genuinely doable for a busy parent!

Finally, working on yourself is one of the best investments you can make for yourself and your children. Having kids pushes us to take a long hard look at ourselves which can be really difficult, especially when old pain re-emerges, for which you may need further professional support. Motherhood also affords us an incredible opportunity to grow as parents and as human beings. All parenting begins with you. In this beautiful book, Geraldine gently guides us through the unraveling of our journeys through motherhood to finding our identities again, so we can begin to work on loving and accepting who we are through the ups and the lows. In her words: *"It is energizing and powerful to uncover our own truth, find ourselves, and unravel"*.

Love and light to you.
Dr. Malie Coyne, clinical psychologist and author of
Love In, Love Out: A Compassionate Approach to Parenting Your Anxious Child

Introduction

SINCE I GAVE BIRTH TO my first child, I have felt this constant pressure to be a dynamic mother. To heal quickly after a caesarean section, to carry on through baby blues, to manage intuitively throughout the first year, and to find my way out of postnatal depression and the intensity of long-term anxiety. It was as though I was asked to stitch myself together with the pressured expectations of motherhood and hide the struggles that were birthed along with a new mothering identity. Amongst it all was the pressure to be a satisfied mother with the answers to life's greatest mysteries, while modelling the ideals of how to raise a happy family, excel in my job, and be my own person. It has been exhausting. All the while my arms have been raised overhead in Mountain Pose as I inhale a deep and longing breath as I attempt to connect with my wants and needs amidst this chaos of family life. And I ran with this idea of a perfect life as a mother, even when it made me feel inadequate.

I somehow expected my life, before nappies and Sudocrem, buggy choices and school possibilities, to merge with rocking it as a mum into one coherent "I got this shit" kind of life. Instead, it was more of a "where did all this shit come from?" kind of life as I charted the contents of my babies' bowels and kept track of whatever Google tried to teach me about its varying color. I dutifully sat in the passenger seat of motherhood, believing that I had no influence on the navigation as I was driven along far too fast in the wrong direction.

The pressure to mother a certain way was as unrelenting as the round ligament pains that brought me into this world of kissing knees, sore hands, and wondering if beans on toast were alright for a Wednesday night dinner. And yes, beans are perfectly ok, because sometimes we need simplicity, good enough, and a bit of melting butter. From the beginning, I was in love with my new role as mum, but also lost. The incredible juxtaposition of motherhood. A constant swaying pendulum of "I love it" and "I can't do this."

Throughout my years as a mother, I debated whether this pressure to be exceptional, or even mediocre with only a winning spark every so often, was because the world spins in a continued drive for nothing but success. Desperate to not get left behind, I sprinted to catch up. I found myself throwing every ball in the air, stretching out my jumper in the hopes that I would catch something, anything, on its way down but by the time our second daughter arrived, I simply could not juggle it all anymore.

Yet, in the beginning, I didn't feel as though I had a choice. Swollen and rotund with our first child growing in my belly, I was still commuting an hour on a stuffy bus, working nine to five, and very much entrenched by my career as a medical librarian in the world's oldest working maternity hospital of all places. I was also suffering intense hyperemesis gravidarum (severe pregnancy sickness) with no reprieve. Still, I barely missed a day of work believing the myth that mothers, and those soon-to-be mothers, carried on, never complained, and accepted their lot.

I was wholly caught up in the world of pregnancy at work, conducting literature searches on pre-eclampsia and shoulder-dystocia. I could rhyme off the current trends in obstetrics and gynecology while quoting from *Mayes Midwifery*. I knew the complications of pregnancy and birth but motherhood, the depth and breadth of its transformation, was not found in any textbook on the library's shelves.

Every working day, for ten years, I would swipe my ID and sidle through the side gate, walk by the gold-gilded frames of the previous hospital Masters, all men, in the ornate front hall of the 250-year-old building. The echo of footsteps mingled with voices, the gentle hum of modernity through the bright lights, and that acute sharp shrill of a hungry infant. These rich and imposing portraits of men who delivered baby after baby hauntingly reminded me of the patriarchy, which upholds our very mothering system and the stereotypes we are born into. And, of course, peering down at me as I shuffled past the canteen, there was the one demanding and authoritative portrait of Sara Hampson, the first lady superintendent of the Rotunda Hospital in 1891. A woman among men, among women, among newborns.

Certainly not lacking in a deep and relevant history, I never imagined that a time would come, and I would ask, "Did every one of those mothers, those ghosts from the hospital's 275-year history, have any inkling of what that bulging belly, suckling baby, and aching body meant for them as women? Did they think the same thoughts as me? Or am I the only mother in the history of the Rotunda to feel like I was doing this all wrong?"

Our eldest daughter, Allegra, was born on a wet and dreary October afternoon, after 15 hours of labor amid a failing induction. In that year, 2013, 8,648 mothers delivered 8,841 babies.[1] All within the same walls as I did. And in 2017, when we added our second and final baby girl, Devin, to our brood after a somewhat difficult pregnancy, 8,226 mothers delivered 8,409 babies.[2] That's a lot of women becoming mothers either for the first time, or again. Every new addition bucks the trend of change in a woman. And this is but one hospital, in one county, in one country. Women merging from their childless years to mothering years, one child years, two or three, or the mother who begins again with newborn days after a gap of many years hoping the older, mature, and doting older child will help carry some of the load. Mothers are born as quickly, painfully, and manically as their children. Transforming and exploring with gain and loss and spit-up on their shoulders. So many women, so much change, and so little conversation surrounding this concentrated transformation.

The inclination to start a family with my husband, Barry, who was tied to me seven years at the time, was almost a by-product of literally that—being married seven years and moving on to the next inevitable stage of our coupling. However, it wasn't as simple as that. As Nell Frizzell so eloquently puts it, I was smack in the middle of The Panic Years.[3] Verging between maintaining life as is or stepping into motherhood, entirely unprepared for either eventuality but knowing in the deepest part of me that my womb, my mind, my life was ready for children because it was time. And not exclusively because I was suggestible and influenced by the doting dads who carried the tiniest of babies in carriers to the car as I ran out the door to catch a bus home to my relaxed and perplexing life. I was not perturbed by the newfound mother who paced unevenly and achingly behind their newborn bundle, clutching at hidden wounds under Disney pajamas.

The idea of motherhood, those panic years of when we should start discussing the option of a family, hit a few years before I became pregnant. It was a vicious assault on my ovaries and suddenly, it was all I could think about. For me, it was now, for him it was later but every year later increased the already complicated nature of pregnancy. For those few years, I readied myself for the practicalities of motherhood and raising babies, while he grew comfortable with the idea of wanting children. But in truth, those panic years did not prepare me for the completely unique and different panic that would set in. I was not prepared for the intense metamorphosis we undergo as women, carers, and nurturing souls when motherhood comes along.

My life and the inner workings of my mind were rocked by the pause of early motherhood, the absence of needing to be anywhere other than on the sofa under a breathing bundle of blankets. Postpartum seemed so alien, so empty, yet entirely all-encompassing. That fourth trimester was temporary… but it was a pause, nonetheless. A much-needed pause and period of intense adjustment. Learning to mother, heal, and everything else that comes with tiny babies and how they significantly change our lives in such a particular and peculiar way with soft cotton, erratically flexing pudgy limbs, and dangerously sharp fingernails. It is, after all, in this pause that we find a reset, an unraveling, and a new perspective. The only thing needed to reach this pause is to be open to it despite the perturbed exhaustion and overwhelm of motherhood.

I did not realize this pause was perhaps one of the most critical times of my life. Not the birth of my child, but the time that comes after when I become the woman I want to be along with this new persona of mother. However, after the pause, life remained confusing, scary, and I was looking for a little direction before the draining fuel tank hit empty.

Balancing work and home, deadlines, and dust, I committed myself to figuring out how to pull off a work suit on a Tuesday, and Lycra leggings on a Thursday, all the while carrying the mental load and fishing a Lego batman out of the toilet. I found myself incredibly organized with a baby bag always stocked and ready to go for those impromptu and drastically necessary "get out of the house" moments yet struggled to get a foot out of the door. I had four bottles of unopened Calpol in a lockable container at the back of the fridge, and I invested in not one but two first aid kits with added Peppa Pig plasters. I was ready for life as a mother and seemed forever clued in on when Aldi had their baby events. I even thought I was ready for round two when the baby morphed into a toddler and the rhythm of living seemed, well, achievable.

But this all-consuming calling of motherhood has cut me down on many a day, and I have wanted to run into the farmer's field opposite our house, bare foot, and scream into the abyss of a dark night sky, willing no one and everyone to hear me. I have yet to do this, but have promised myself one day, I will roar. Just like a good cry, a decent earth-shattering howl seems needed and wholly justified.

Since becoming the proud owner of two highly opinionated, fast, and confusing children, it is safe to say I have slowly but surely lost a whole heap of days and thoughts in the blur of motherhood, and a few dinners along the way. I love the dirt on their faces, the knots in their hair, and the way they pick the fluff out of their toes every time they take their socks off, but this conversation is not about our love, our devotion or commitment to parenting and genuinely doing our best by our children. It is about filling our own cup, loving ourselves and being wholly and comprehensively aware of ourselves and the torrent of emotion motherhood quietly and impudently delivers to us. I have felt lost and overwhelmed, completely tangled, and disagreeable about the whole idea of motherhood. I raced ahead and left my role as a librarian and moved on to work from home as a journalist and writer, albeit under a Crayola stain. I have thrown up flashcards in front of my baby, fearfully watched the washing machine spin as the favorite teddy spins around and ticked my way through the list of things I believed had to be done to show the world I was getting along simply fine, achieving. However, at the same time, I was silently asking, "Is this it? Is this motherhood?"

I once described my kids as two deliriously mixed-up Rubik cubes. A puzzle I tackled every day, solving one side as quickly as I mixed up another. The more I twisted, rotated, and tried to win at this game, the faster I lost and fell into frustration, balancing on the brink of burnout. Postnatal depression and a hefty side order of postnatal anxiety, which I tartly refer to as my Fricking Flamingo, shattered me to my core after Devin with her head of blonde hair made her appearance. The Flamingo ungracefully flew into my life, creating a personal shit storm at a time when I was told I was so lucky and must be so happy, and my god, can you stand the cuteness of it all?

I found I could move through twenty different emotions in five minutes, recognizing, appreciating, and consolidating them all while remaining calm, reserved and in control and then suddenly, poof. The Flamingo twisted the rationale of my mind and I struggled to hold it together, losing it with explosive, unrecognizable feelings and reactions, and a sickness and tightness in my chest that attempted to burst through my ribcage. The Flamingo manically flapped its wings and flipped my emotions, silencing any rational thought, shattering my physical and mental responses so loudly and frighteningly that my insides shook. I didn't recognize myself and felt so tremendously knotted.

Postnatal depression and anxiety became mingled with that awkward pull between investing in myself as a mother and simultaneously hating the responsibility of parenthood. I was stuck between loving my kids so painfully but wanting to disappear. I felt an urge to find my maternal groove but desperately wanted to stay completely and solidly the person I was beginning to miss. I was simultaneously ugly crying and snorting with laughter and utterly tangled up in the confusion of motherhood and life and expectations and all of the new emotions.

It was the mother-me versus the me-me that caused the cracking of my mental health and the puzzle of how to parent two kids. There was no denying that I was this mother person, and she was me, jumbled with a multitude of fragmentary shattered pieces, never feeling complete.

I figured my kids were the puzzle, so it took quite a lot of twisting before I realized it was me who was mixed up, needing the stickers to be picked off and rearranged. I was free-falling with all the weight and motherly expectations pushing me down. I was guilty with the belief I was wrong, unduly agonizing over the right way to parent, desperately reaching for anything to pull me out of my frustrated head, and questioning what I really had to complain about? How could this period of my life be so challenging, off center, and alien to me when it was meant to be my revolution, my dream, a wild new beginning? Wasn't I craving the anarchy and intrigue of modern family life? Isn't this what I wanted? What was wrong with me?

You see, this modern age of motherhood puts pressure on us to be enterprising, fearless, resourceful, to do more, and be more, forgetting we are human and learning and brimming with feelings, thoughts, dreams, and desires. But for a long time, I never felt I could hit the mark I assumed I was supposed to, wondering was I holding myself back or was it the Flamingo?

And yet, like everyone else, I would keep going, aiming higher than I needed, and constantly believe I was failing or falling or tripping up. I felt as though I was missing the mark as the mother earth who supposedly doesn't need to think twice about how well she is raising her kids, or the super-mum who evidently never complains and carries on tick, tick, ticking her way through the list, or as the highly sensitive and aware mother who monitors and balances the emotions and needs of everyone in the house, including the dog and Jasper the goldfish. I was exhausted by it all, wondering "do these women even exist?" when all I wanted to do was eat my weight in doughnuts. Not even the fancy kind of doughnuts that are an overpriced, indulgent pleasure. Plain old sugar and jam would do.

As I tried to be someone I wasn't, battling an internal conflict, I doubted myself 89 times in the day. As the kids fell asleep, I quietly apologized to them for when I was a grumpy mum, a tired mum, or a wrong mum. I have felt contemptuous guilt as I collected the half-eaten dinners of waffles and cheese and promised myself that tomorrow I would get them to eat broccoli, even though I knew the broccoli would stay in the freezer aisle in the supermarket for another mum to throw into her cart. I would tell myself, when they travel the world, they will try sushi which will make up for those early years of a bad diet.

I'm not a perfect mother. I don't always get it right. I have made mistakes, but at the end of the day, when those eyes close and they gently breathe the slow rhythmic song of comfortable sleep, all I need to know is that they are happy, that I tried my best, and that tomorrow I will try again.

Motherhood has been a journey of self-discovery as I listened to my thoughts, emotions, reasoning's, wants, needs, desires, and began to understand what it means to feel complete. I have allowed myself to unravel one day at a time.

There is so much more to mothering than I realized in those beginning days—years!—of parenthood, so much loss mixed in with the gain. It is not simply about mothering our children, but also ourselves, every single day. We are almost blindsided into simply accepting this intense change, ignoring the markings it leaves, and getting on with it because we are not the first to bear a child, not the first to find ourselves changed and confused and longing. We are not told that birthing a child is an individual revolution, a personal awakening, or reawakening, and we are not warned how savagely we will need to adjust, inside and out. Priorities change. Love changes. We grow up a little more. We let go of standards, play the floor is lava, and almost always put our needs second. OK, third. OK, our needs are often dropped by the sideboard of lost intentions, only to be remembered as we fall into bed or sit on the loo with an audience.

Mothering is not a straight line. It jolts up, slides down and sometimes sways sideways. But we learn from our days. Things we said we would never do are revisited. Ideas we had for the future, fragment and refine.

I had an extreme lack of clarity on my life, let alone my motherhood, when the Flamingo landed. And yet, despite being crippled with thirty or more anxiety attacks a day, I found myself questioning my life. It got to a point where I needed to unravel my insides and stitch myself back together from my inner core outward. I was guided through counselling, mindfulness, self-awareness, and so much more towards a pattern to knit myself back up, helping me mend those dropped stitches. There's been quite a lot of sewing up, and there are some awkward knots which have yet to loosen because I'm still learning and changing and unraveling. I expect to continue this process for most of my life because none of this is linear. We will continually change as our children grow.

In many ways, motherhood asks us to look outside of ourselves as we begin to unravel, yet also requires, so profoundly and heavily, attention to what is within ourselves. It asks us to understand the intensity inside our minds which translates into our actions, to understand this baffling and unspoken transformation into the glorious woven empire of motherhood, to recover and uncover who we are, who we will become and what that means in the context of who we want to be.

Unraveling is frightening, complicated, messy, and confusing. There is no greater change than becoming a mother. It took me two children and three years of damaged mental wellbeing before I reconciled with mothering, with me, with all of the emotions, thoughts, questions, and painful conversations I have had with myself in order to believe in myself.

Unraveling is good. Stitching up is better. When the pattern is not working out the way we were hoping, we must first unravel to start again.

How To Use This Book

● **Unravel** \ ən-ˈra-vəl \

to resolve the intricacy, complexity, or obscurity of; clear up

Dictionary, **Merriam-Webster**

M Y INTENTION FOR YOU throughout this book is to actively travel with you throughout a journey of critical self-reflection to uncover a positive self-awareness. In this way, we can unravel, separate, and understand those thoughts and feelings that block us from connecting with the women and mothers that we are. We will challenge the assumptions and beliefs we have about motherhood, about ourselves, and find meaningful perspectives on our life as a mother to understand our inner selves more deeply.

I have nothing to gain by being insincere about motherhood, smoothing over the cracks or throwing glitter on the more challenging days. You have nothing to gain by yet another undiscerning conversation about baby smiles, cute farts, and the oddly embracing scent of warm milk. For too long, we have swept the tough parts under the rug in the hope no one notices the difficult truth that motherhood is not perfect. That is why, this book, at times is raw in its honesty, which makes it truthful in its reality because I am an open book to you. I cannot expect you to open yourself up unless I show you the worth in our sincerity and our vulnerability. Through unraveling, we can find our own truth, identity, and purpose to live a profound and fulfilled life during the many intensely exhausting and overwhelming periods of motherhood. This sounds so simple, prosaic, and superfluous, but it is a culmination of our very core, our day-to-day routine, newsfeeds, shopping lists, thoughts and dreams, and a reinterpretation of the world imposing on us.

By actively reflecting and becoming aware of our inner thoughts and the world around us, we can do our best to counter that which can negatively impact our beliefs about mothering and ourselves. Through mindfulness, meditation, critical thinking, sinking into fiction, plenty of TV with your preferred tea, some yoga, scribbling, anything you are comfortable with and satisfied by, and deep self-awareness, we can reimagine motherhood.

This conversation we are about to have is about you—the inner you, which only you can hear. *Listen* to her, as you read these pages. Listen to what she wants, needs, what she loves, and why she agrees or disagrees with what we will discuss. Truly listen to her because it is her voice we need to unravel.

That being said, you do not need to be a new mother to benefit from this book. These emotions and thought patterns we strive to work through are not exclusive to new motherhood and can occur at any stage of the mothering journey. Nor are they limited solely to those who have personally given birth—any person who identifies as a mother or fulfills that role in someone's life can find solace and aid in these pages. The flow of this book has been crafted to support any mother, in whatever manner she became a mother, at any stage of her emotional growth. And boy, is there a lot of growth! Learning about ourselves never ends as we tackle each stage and transitional moment of motherhood and raising children.

Many aspects within these chapters may help to navigate post-natal depression, anxiety, the emotional and physical overwhelm of motherhood, and those questions we sometimes feel we cannot ask aloud. Mental health is not an overbearing theme or consideration within this book, mainly because our mental wellbeing is all-encompassing in motherhood, but psychological gravity weighs heavily through our life and, as such, mothering. However, having worn the path of postnatal depression and anxiety, it would be remiss of me to preclude this conversation with the understanding that this book is not a substitute for the help we as mothers may need. Please remember to seek support and help from your GP, midwife, Public Health Nurse, family, and close friends if you find your emotions are overwhelming or your thoughts are obtrusive. Delving deeper into your core beliefs about yourself and the world you find yourself in, is best done in the safe hands of a qualified therapist.

This is one reason why there are discussions within each chapter with psychologists and professionals on topics I am not qualified to unravel. I swear by their support, understanding, and completely non-judgmental approach in helping us figure out our mind's inner workings. I have actively taken on board their expertise and advice in putting these chapters together. There will also be a flourish of exercises about self-reflection, understanding, and self-awareness, as well as questions and lists because lists are ultimately satisfying.

The purpose of *Unraveling Motherhood* is to recognize how mothers are influenced to mother a certain way, discern the outside influences that can alter our thinking, and find an inner strength to listen and trust ourselves. Also, to remember our individuality, to care for ourselves, and to love the mothers and women we are. It is very much an evolving, consistent, and thought-provoking existence that needs continual exploration. Even as I write these chapters, I am going through a second revolution within my own thoughts and practices as my children grow into early independence. We are continually growing and always learning as our kids do.

It is helpful to do the exercises scattered throughout the book in a notebook as we will be doing a lot of thinking, writing, and bringing to the surface of these thoughts as we go along. If you're like me, you may like to choose a beautiful journal or notebook that speaks to you. Something that is yours to intentionally rant and rave, dissect and autopsy, to scribble and scrawl in and to unearth your own primary revolution.

There may be elements within this book you feel are not relevant to you. Still, I urge you to read the discussions and reflect on the exercises as you never know what feelings or thoughts may be buried within you and when released, may be vitally empowering for you. It is energizing and powerful to uncover our own truth, find ourselves, and unravel.

There are a few things I would like you to remember as we kick start this journey:

1: You are not broken.

Motherhood stings with a powerful broad spectrum of intense emotions which fluctuate and contradict each other. It can make us question why we feel a certain way which seems to go against the norm. As though we are wrong or fractured somehow. We are not broken. We are not trying to "fix" ourselves with all this unraveling but rather understand ourselves and all the emotions we feel.

Every. Single. Emotion. Is. Valid.

I cannot emphasize this enough. You will see this idea filtered throughout the book because we are not fighting against our emotions. We are empowering ourselves. We are not damaged or flawed. We are human.

2: You are not ungrateful.

We are allowed to recognize when something is not happening the way we envisioned. Recognizing the shortcomings does not make us ungrateful for all we have. As we guide ourselves through this important process of self-reflection, be kind to yourself and know that changing your outlook, searching for yourself, sometimes resenting the "job", and having strong emotions and thoughts is freeing. You can be grateful and look for change and growth.

3: You are enough.

You truly are.

chapter 1

Unraveling Clichés

● **Clichés** \ klē-'shā /
something that has become overly familiar or commonplace
Dictionary, **Merriam-Webster**

WHAT IS MOTHERHOOD? OVER the decades we have severely complicated this most natural and instinctual role, wrapped it up into boxes and marked it with thick black permanent marker as motherhood complied with being explicitly a social role bounded by culture and society. Labelled as a young mother, a first-time mother, a working mother, an older mother, a distracted mother, hands-on mother, perfectionist mother, the list goes on but you and I both know, we cannot fit the intensity of rearing our children under a few labels, attach it to an ideal or societal expectation, or allow it to flow with overused clichés.

Motherhood is not something to be boxed or pigeonholed into a category or an idea. It is complex, contradictory, and individual. As we are going to jump straight in and unravel our ideas around being a mother, we must step outside of these boxes, rewrite or reject the labels, and create our own understanding of being mum. We're not looking for limp, derailing definitions which ignore the magnificence of this experience and the wholly universal subject that it is, nor are we looking for that overcomplicated theory behind the nature and history of the mothering mind.

We are looking for what all of this means to us, personally, because every one of us will have a different understanding and when it's all laid out with the talcum powder and rusks, we can make our own judgement, and be comfortable with it.

But where do we begin with unraveling an idea as big as motherhood?

We can start with what we know, what we are told, the anecdotes that make up what a "good mother" is, the stories that are fed to us from the myths, clichés, and ideologies of motherhood. Because to find out what we believe in, we can begin questioning that which is out of place.

Myths, Clichés, Ideologies

Admittedly, starting this discussion on such a heavy topic was not what I intended, but as I delved deeper into our assumptions about mother-hood, I could not ignore the expectations of motherhood that impact on how we view ourselves. Considering these ideologies may be all we know of motherhood, why should we question them? Largely because they are dated, contrived, and irregular philosophies containing almost nothing that we can relate to. And this is why answering the question, "What is motherhood?" is so tricky.

The many myths, clichés and ideologies surrounding motherhood sell a bias that most certainly fails to fit in with our own ideas and percep-tions. The promotion of prominent traditional cultural values filters its way into our minds as we grow from young girls to adults with images of being a nurturing, self-sacrificing, content, and gracious mother. These ideas come without argument, purpose, or rational thought as to the reality of what we may experience.

There is the *Gender Ideology* that conveys the traditional gender roles of parenthood and assumes that women become the primary caregiver by remaining in the home while a male partner works outside of the home. The *Good Mother Ideology* that supposes motherhood comes naturally to women and the perceived societal rules around motherhood are not broken. The *Life's Purpose Ideology* that proposes an expectation that our primary concern is to care for our family above all else.[1, 2]

The myths, clichés, and ideologies which deliver these unconscious assumptions need to be challenged so we can form our own empowering path. To do so, we need to detangle ourselves from the constraints of a patriarchal belief of motherhood and allow ourselves to be the women and mothers we want to be.

When we become mothers, it's no wonder we may ask, "Is this it?" Questioning our role, and why we are offered an unrecognizable motherhood culture, is one of the first steps to understanding and owning our motherhood. If we do not relate to the ideas we are shown, do we question our truth? Do we believe what we are sold and change our behaviors to suit that ideal? Do we staunchly defy the ideology of others and commit to what we personally believe? Or do we battle between the two, leading us to consistently question who we are as mothers, and why we mother the way we do, battling self-criticism?

We are taught from an early age that motherhood is our expected female life cycle. That motherhood is about self-sacrifice (making self-care selfish), it's our job to run the home, breastfeeding comes naturally, bonding is instantaneous, motherhood is completely fulfilling, motherhood is exhausting and involves copious amounts of wine, a good mother never shouts, and if motherhood is not enough for you, you're not doing it right. However, the maternal experience is complex and varied with ambivalence, frustration, and high expectations.

I shout. I struggled to breastfeed. I despise wine. I didn't bond with my first child until she was about a year old, and I am not fulfilled by motherhood but rather by my dreams and aspirations. So, where do I fall in these mothering beliefs? Does it make me a bad mother? Am I failing?

If the discussion around motherhood, especially in popular culture, comes across as unrelatable and a mythical construct, how are we to find ourselves in the scenario? We are left feeling inadequate and unable, stifled in guilt, shame or as though there is something wrong with us.

Detaching Myth from Reality

Our definition of motherhood is outside of the boundaries of the myths, clichés, and ideals that we grow up with. Yes, we may very well experience every cliché of motherhood at some stage or another—the exhaustion, the focused conversations that barely spill outside of our children's lives, knowing that "this too shall pass"—but they do not epitomize what motherhood means for us. While the clichés are rife, they will not always ring true for us, because this overall experience of motherhood is so much greater than the stories we are told. It is an internal experience which has us unraveling to our core, has made us question so many things about who we are, why we feel the way we do, and why the echo in the silence of this conversation is so loud.

Motherhood herself was not something I gave a second thought to, even as I pulled the deliriously wonderful elasticated waistband over my protruding belly. I had somehow expected it to simply become a part of my life. When I had our first child, Allegra, at the age of thirty, I expected everything to fall into place. I didn't understand how nuanced motherhood really is. While I was so in love with this baby who needed me, I didn't feel the expected maternal connection, nor was I assured by the knowledge that I was necessary in her life. Anyone could care for her. What could I give her that others couldn't?

I had a few friends who had already ventured into the world of Babygro's and cot mobiles, and they seemed to effortlessly battle the load I knew nothing about. I was a terrified new mum but didn't realize it until self-doubt showed her face as I counted the ounces of milk left in the bottle. With every day I became more knotted in my motherhood.

I was hollowed out and hidden as I held my daughter, feeling no connection to her or my ability to be her primary carer. I was overwhelmed and underwhelmed by the whole experience. So much so, I allowed others to take over my baby, in many ways detaching myself even further from learning anything about this incredible transformation into motherhood. I stood on the side-lines of motherhood despite having grown and birthed this tiny human being. She was mine, yet I could barely mother her, bond with her, or trust myself with her from the very beginning. I allowed strangers to pick up my baby, friends to stick their thumb into her mouth to suck on, relatives to change her clean clothes, wake her up, rock her, burp her, feed her, and encourage her to walk, smile, talk, and eventually sing, while I was out of the room. All which may seem trivial in the grand scheme of things, but when I look back on that first year of motherhood I am saddened by the fear, lack of confidence, and distance I allowed in that first step into this lifetime job.

In that first year, that overwhelming belief that I was already failing sat with me as I folded the laundry, tickled her belly, and mashed her banana. I didn't challenge my beliefs. I didn't unravel them because I didn't know I could.

Unravel

What are the clichés, myths, and ideologies you are holding on to? In your journal or here on these pages, think about the following:

What are some of the ideas of motherhood which seem to be common-place but are not relevant to you? For example, do you believe the myth that a "good mother" knows how to instinctively care for her baby?

_____

_____

_____

Think about how these clichés or ideas make you feel about yourself. Do you feel guilty, ashamed, worthless, not up to scratch?

_____

_____

_____

Do you need to conform to these ideas of motherhood, or can you let them go?

_____

_____

_____

Unravel

Debunking the myths is always tricky considering it becomes a myth or cliché when it is repeated and thereby believed by many. When something feels familiar, it feels true. It's how fake news runs riot!

There are a few questions we can ask when a perceived notion about motherhood gets us all knotted up:

- Do others believe it? And if so, does it feel familiar?
- Is there much supporting evidence showing this to be true? Or is the evidence hearsay?
- Does it align with what I believe in? Does it make me uncomfortable? Is it difficult to process, understand, and relate to?
- Does it make logical sense?
- And where did this belief come from?

The added difficulty in debunking any myths surrounding motherhood is that when we bust a myth we feel as though we are creating controversy because we are "going against convention." Remembering that there is no single way to mother is an important facet to continually remind yourself of. The old adage of "You do you" should come before any ideal, standard, or myth.

I pondered questions like, "Why do I feel so empty?" "Why is motherhood no longer calling to me?" and "What am I doing wrong, that I can't seem to connect with the need to be a mother?" Of course, I wasn't asking to suddenly fit a label or match with an ideal identity; most of us don't want that. Our minds are filled with our own unique ideas, dreams, and imaginations of what being a mother will be like. We have a yearning to figure out how to get along with that mother, find her, appreciate her, and love her.

We may fight against our motherhood self, thinking she is the thing that is breaking us away from the person we already know and love. However, retaliating against her will bring us further away from ourselves. She is a part of us. She's pretty damn fierce, ferocious, protective, and creative. The fact that she is a surprise invader after the extra toes and fingers come into the house, makes it a little harder to gravitate toward her at the beginning. And she comes with those preconceived notions and assumptions about what it means to be mum.

Describing my own personal idea of motherhood, in all its "pick n' mix" glory, was a starting point for me as I felt stuck in a world I was battling against. The ideals that society told me to relate to, grated against how I actually mothered, but my lack of confidence and poor self-belief told me to ignore myself and listen to the "experts."

Feeling lost in motherhood is one of the most common conversations we have as women. The transformation is much like a birth. We are reborn but there is no one there to mother us during this transition. When we begin to think about motherhood in all of her bare-naked glory, pick at her spots, and pluck her hairs, we learn so much about ourselves. Step one in unraveling is to describe our understanding of motherhood.

Understanding Motherhood

To avoid the trappings and falling for the clichés which do nothing to help us figure out who we want to be while raising and loving our children, I encourage you to be open in your understanding and listen to yourself amid the chaos and explosion of theories, projections, ideologies and thought patterns. The idea throughout all of this is to find your truth. Listen to your own mind, your thoughts, and the sensations that arise in you as we explore ourselves.

Understanding motherhood is too large of a concept to work through in one chapter. It is so delinquently smashed into fragments, that we need to tackle it slowly. So, we will gently unravel it, thread by thread, emotion by emotion, thought by thought, throughout the next seven chapters. And hopefully by the final chapter, *Stitching Up,* we can knit all these thoughts and feelings together to create our own relevant truth in understanding our motherhood, our way of mothering, and most importantly, ourselves.

Looking at the bigger picture of our life and the all-encompassing concept of motherhood, we can begin to understand our reactions, emotions, beliefs, and values and how they can merge with our mothering path. We can center our awareness and wellbeing to uncover our identity and core values. And drink coffee because we love the taste and not because we're told we need it.

Reflecting on Motherhood

Reflecting on what motherhood means to you is a good place to begin. You may feel a confusion and misgiving in your thought patterns surrounding your idea of motherhood and want to skip this exercise which is why I've kept it simple. Trusting your thoughts, decisions, and beliefs is the beginning of understanding.

So, we ask:

- What is motherhood for us?

- What do we want to get out of motherhood?

- What are our expectations?

- Why are we doing this?

- Are we enjoying it?

- Why do we feel the way we do?

- Who do we want to be?

You do not need to try to answer these questions just yet. They are ideas floating in our mind, questions biting at us on our anxious days, exhausted days, vulnerable days, empty days. They are not questions, or ideas we can simply answer off the top of our head in one sentence or thought anyway. They may not even be questions we can answer by the end of this chapter or even the end of this book. The first year of motherhood may slowly but quickly disappear, the second, the fifth, and you may still wonder what being a mother truly means to you. And that's ok.

So, let's simplify this exercise by using five simple words.

Unravel

Let's pause for a moment and consider how to unravel the definition of motherhood in three expanded forms. Motherhood as an ideology, you as mother, and you as you. Consider the traits, characteristics, qualities, feelings, and values you associate with each form.

Reflecting outside of the realms of the clichés, the influences, and the projections of others, look deep within yourself and listen to your thoughts as you consider your motherhood journey. Focus on what is in the forefront of your mind whether it is positive or negative. Be patient if the words don't come, and if you can't find five words for each, that is perfectly ok. We may not know how to describe our thoughts yet, but we will find the right words eventually.

Write down five words which describe motherhood.

_____

_____

_____

Write down five words which describe you as mother.

_____

_____

_____

(continued next page)

Write down five words which describe you.

_____

_____

_____

If you found this exercise difficult, don't worry. We are ultimately raw at this stage of unraveling in both mind and heart. If you jotted down words which seem negative or upsetting, that's ok too. Remember that we are at the beginning of this journey of rediscovery, of understanding. We will not have all the answers at this stage. This state of flux which motherhood has us whirling in is a complicated, messy, and organic whirlwind. It requires care and attention, as does your mind. So, as we are guided through these pages to face questions, interpret thoughts, and open the conversation of motherhood, be gentle with yourself.

Every word you write, every thought you have, every question you ask on this journey, is valid.

Expectations vs Reality

Naive and unsure as to what daily life with kids would be like, I walked into the unknown with the idea of perfect, happy families. Expectations of warm baby cuddles, rainy day arts and crafts, and the calm serenity of a baby without silent reflux or one who refused to sleep when the sun goes down. I was ill prepared for the struggles and monotony of daily life, forgetting that the picture in my head was an ideal.

As the expectations started to grow, and my mind fled to decorating the nursery, maxing my credit card, and wondering whether or not to find out the gender, I didn't give a passing thought to the possibility of a caesarean section (which of course happened, twice), or postnatal depression (which also happened, twice), or the isolation, the self-doubt, or how many arms I would need to grow to manage the overwhelm. I didn't ponder the clash between working life and mothering life, between my identity and a newfound personality who interrupted the life I was used to.

It's unfair to suggest that our unrealistic expectations of motherhood are entirely our own fault. How are we to have any inkling of what any of this entails until we are knee deep in it all? Our expectations disappear into the background of teething rings in the freezer and Babygro's desperately drying near the radiator. We are not aware that societal ideals, media expectation, and our social feeds create an unrealistic dream of motherhood, pressuring us to be creative, organized, and always loving life.

Let's not forget our past. How we were parented, the values our parents have and instilled in us, and our memories of our childhood, our teenage years and even now as adults, influence our beliefs. The interactions we had with our parents leave a lasting core message.

The Parenting Cycle

In many ways, my idea of motherhood was the childhood version of my own mother who was wrapped up with three children as a stay-at-home mother in a recession in the 80's. It is not exactly something my own experience could relate to. I am a working mother with a blend of the home office and parenting with complications from overpowering technology and intrusive influences. However, that 1980s vision was all I really knew of motherhood, and she seemed to make it look so easy through my inexperienced eyes.

I know my idea of my mum is blurred, and I know her days were hard, that she could write the book on loneliness, frustration, sad days, happy days, achievements, and cock ups. But I remember the mum who bought me popcorn after swimming lessons and walked the twenty-minute stretch with me to catch the bus to the pool every Saturday morning in miserable rain. The mum who was relieved when I asked to quit ballet but proud when she saw me dance on stage. I remember the mum who had movie nights prepared for us after school and let us lick the icing bowl once the buns were sufficiently iced. The mum who always, without fail, helped me fall back asleep at 3 am and tucked me in with a hug and kiss and a safety blanket of happiness. My relationship with my parents is thankfully solid, and I appreciate the experiences they gave me and the memories that I contentedly and warmly relive. Their support and guidance have played a deliberate role in how I parent now after I unraveled many knots, but consequently in those earlier years I assumed it all should have been so much easier than it actually was.

I was aware my mother suffered postnatal depression, that my father hit burnout at work, but the effect their sacrifices and setbacks had on me were very much buried until I had my own children. In essence, we very much learn to parent by our past experiences, our relationships, and our parents' values. Our own childhoods reside in our minds as we follow the path into motherhood ourselves. We either mirror or reject these values, experiences, and encounters, as we find our own path. Reflecting on our relationship with our parents, their values, and how they parented us can help us to understand our own values.

Unravel

Let's pause and consider how our parents reared us and if that has an influence on how we parent. Take some time to consider the following questions. Using your notebook, jot down words, phrases, or even doodles which conjure up ideas and answers to these questions.

- What was your childhood like?
- Describe your relationship with your mother?
- What are your mother's values?
- Describe your relationship with your father?
- What are your father's values?
- What was the most difficult thing about your childhood?
- Describe a happy moment from your childhood?
- How did your parents talk and communicate with you?
- If you could go back and change anything about your childhood, what would you change?
- How do you think your childhood influenced your adult life?

Ideology of Motherhood

Detaching the myth, the clichés, and the platitudes of motherhood from the realities can be quite a disheartening experience. We find ourselves embracing our baby, our minds full of visions that don't match our own and leave us wondering where we went wrong. Unsurprisingly, we blame ourselves.

The issue here is not that we are wrong but that we have not recognized our own reality. Consequently, we feel cheated out of an idea that seems to be exactly what we looked forward to. And therein lie the perils of the myth.

Naturally, the expectation versus reality argument will fall on different levels for every person. The ideas we have, our past experiences, and how we identify as mothers, all play a part in our own personal beliefs. These patterns of belief enable us to find a suitable place to sit at the table. They help us to create identities, give value to our lives, and often empower us to characterize ourselves and each other in either positive or negative ways. This is not always helpful as we internalize ideologies which may not be constructive to us or those around us, creating a battle at the core of our beliefs.

Let's push deeper into this idea of the motherhood myth to see if we can find ourselves anywhere within it.

The Mother War

We are heavily concerned by the media cycle and are persuaded by the myriad of clichés which envelope motherhood in its various highlight reels online. Expectation versus reality hit me in a slow, delirious, and upsetting way as I fell into a rabbit hole of Instagram performance. Soon enough, I could not find myself anywhere in motherhood. I could not create my own understanding of it amid the blur of life, and I became invisible to myself, aiming for something I could not reach.

If we look at the *Maternal Bliss Myth,* we are met with an ideology that is more than simply being happy with our lot and making sacrifices. It is a hyper ideology surrounding motherhood pertaining to the belief that every woman's aspiration is to be a mother and to give her whole being to the role. It perpetuates the patriarchal system by which a woman is portrayed as the ideal stay-at-home, middle-class mother who is fulfilled by being solely a mother in the private home. It denies her an identity outside of the home and her children, and any unhappiness is attributed to her own failure as a mother.[3]

Somewhat related, we have the *Good Mother Myth*. Another ideal developed from the patriarchy. A mother so perfectly accepting of every small change in motherhood, she is patient, calm, loving, and provides the best care. This quick to love, slow to anger mother plays on a field of her own making, literally with the green paint and perfect chalk lines. She is the most revered mother for all she seems to achieve, and she is happy as she micromanages her children's lives while fueling moral panics within the "good mother" identity. All the while, she is astutely under intensive expectations with unrealistic and significant pressure.[4]

The Goddess Myth battles the *Superwoman Myth* for the top title as both set out to achieve the same result in different, supposedly inspiring ways. One pours her entire spirit into the raising of her children in an applaudable, self-sacrificing manner through the dedication of her entire being to her family. While the other excels in the balancing of a work ethic alongside managing family, home, and relationships.

We have the *Intensive Mothering Myth* which is a supposed perfectly child-centered, labor intensive, and emotionally exhausting ideology attributing mothers to the sole responsibility of the nurture and care of their children. This carries a form of work-family conflict insinuating that the demands of work and family roles are incompatible with each other, which amplifies the motherhood penalty, a subtle and not so subtle discrimination of mothers' experience at work.[5]

In all these myths, the mothers' needs are below those of the child, the home, and the greater good of family. It devolves a woman's life to obligation within unrealistic expectations, which can take a significant toll on our mental wellbeing.

These outdated ideas are still sold within the contemporary motherhood ideology. Our freedom of choice to mother a certain way is our responsibility, meaning the results which come from such a choice are of our own making. Our self-sacrifice is our own. Our overwhelm is our own. Our blame is our own. Our anger and frustration are our own.

This message is inherently flawed because the ideologies are unattainable and unrealistic. Myths tells us that if being a mother is too difficult, if we are not enjoying it, if we are not fulfilled, then we are doing something wrong. Ideologies enforce that being a mother is natural, that we should accept our lot and give up our identity and ambitions. These clichés reiterate that being a mother is natural and instinctual and that if we are struggling, then it is our own fault.

Now, how can that be right?

Unraveling the Myths

Although powerful, many of these myths and clichés are unbalanced with contradictions. We are told the blissful mother agonizes over suspected boredom, confusion, and battles overwhelm. We are told the superwoman is exhausted, guilty, and neglectful. And yet, we are being told one, or the other, is more appropriate and something we, as women, should endeavor to meet. The in-between, the authenticity, and the balance of mothering is stifled in the myths, generating feelings of guilt and inadequacy, and undermining our confidence.[6]

The reality is, many of us don't feel comfortable positioning ourselves along one idea or another. We cannot fit ourselves into a box full of unbalanced ideas, enforced by men to be lived by women. As we look outside of the ideologies of motherhood, we see it as less of a natural event and more as a complex experience which can lead to a distinctive crisis in a woman's life.

The birth of a child is a time for mothers to reparent themselves, reorganize their lives, and relearn their identities. When we shatter these ideas of the all-encompassing mother, we can step outside of the boundaries of these indeterminate ideas and uncover who we are becoming.

Unravel

Let's pause to consider how to unravel these ideologies.

Write out a few expectations you had about motherhood, ideas which seemed plausible and attainable at the time.

_____

_____

_____

Now, write out a few personal examples of being a good mother, whatever "good" means to you, and focus on these messages, personal insights, and expectations, rather than the myths we have anticipated.

_____

_____

_____

It is only when we start to question our expectations that we can begin to construct the idea of our personal motherhood.

So, can we now begin to unravel motherhood in line with our core beliefs, our identity? First, let's understand the complex transition into motherhood, how it affects our mind, our bodies, and our belief in ourselves.

Unraveling the Transition

Even when I was pregnant with my first daughter, I didn't give any thought to how I could figure all of this out. At that stage, I believed this was the next phase of my life after marriage, some solid years of a child free life, and now reproduction. I hated being pregnant. It was difficult, riddled with complications. So much so, my obstetrician told me that my body was not suited to pregnancy! Because of these difficulties, I was consumed by the thought of simply getting through the pregnancy and diving headfirst into caring for that bundle of blankets in my arms. How hard could it be?

Very, it turns out. But alongside caring for a newborn, growing toddlers, and sprouting children, I was not told how to care for myself through the maddening days of minding everyone else's toilet habits, rumbling bellies, and confused emotions. Where do we stand amongst the mayhem of family life?

We begin to grapple with these questions earlier than we realize. Our minds and bodies consistently challenge the rhetoric surrounding motherhood. From the very beginning, from the moment our body breathtakingly gives birth in whatever manner it can or by whatever means motherhood comes to us, we change and question, and diverge into motherhood. Chances are, none of us are intrinsically listening at this point, however. We are exhausted, overwhelmed, and possibly confused. We are learning by being thrown in at the deep end and being "mother" without knowing who the hell she is. We are expected to gracefully adjust our routines, our lives, and our mindset while knowing how to feed, clothe, and burp a baby. There are still days, quite a lot of them, when I don't feel like the adult in this Momma Bear, Baby Bear scenario. When I look at my kids, it is sometimes surreal to think that they are mine, that the adult version of me grew them, birthed them, and has raised them to the point of no longer being babies or toddlers.

As we attempt to unearth some truth about ourselves and our beliefs surrounding motherhood at this early stage, we should try to understand that there is no single definition attributable to motherhood. There is no classification or complicit meaning. We are all diverse people, living varied lives with an untold number of fluctuating conditions which not only make us into the people we are, but determine how we parent.

Motherhood is almost an affliction that rewires the internal mechanisms of our body and brain. Like a switch, sometimes automatically flicked the instant our baby takes their first breath. Except, it is not always the case that as soon as a baby is born, a mother is born too. It certainly wasn't the case for me. My inane lack of self-confidence made me question everything I did with Allegra. My revolution hit when Devin was born, and I refused to feel the same way I did the first time around. However, despite my determination, my mental health was significantly challenged. I felt as though I won as I overcame postnatal anxiety to a point of regaining myself. Having learned an untold amount about myself in this transition, I have been reborn as the mother I longed to be.

Birthing a baby does not necessarily mean we automatically download the parenting gene and move with a maternal grace like Mother Nature intended. This change, while it can be as instantaneous as that light switch for some, it can also occur over time for others. For both, it is a tremendous makeover. Excellently referred to as *Matrescence,* it is an odd meandering of trials, most of which blindside us, which is why this early transformation is so important as we process our way into motherhood.

Matrescence

Matrescence is a brilliant word coined by the anthropologist Dana Raphael in the mid-1970s to describe this psychological motherhood awakening. The reason I like it so much is because it validates a period of our lives as something real and tangible. It re-establishes the focus on us, as women and mothers, and not simply carriers, or machines procreating as is our clichéd "purpose." Matrescence is the shift towards motherhood in all its trials and glories. Considered our psychological birth, if you will, into motherhood.

Let's bear in mind that Matrescence is a state of flux, and it may never end. Although, quite like adolescence, during this time, we are fluctuating in mind and body. Our hormones are delirious, our body ever-changing, and our identity on the cliff edge as we are devoured and spat out by the erratic nature of motherhood. It is a learning, a rebirth, and a growth as we make our way to finding a new, extraordinary strength within us. Yet, this period is largely disorienting, challenging, and not too well discussed on the motherhood boards.

The fourth trimester, the lesser discussed trimester, is the time from birth to about twelve weeks when mother and baby are quite naturally still considered one despite breathing separately. This final trimester, however, is largely concerned with the newborn rather than the mother.

When we consider the raw and incredible change a baby experiences as they find themselves pulled from the safe, comfortable space they knew, we can appreciate how radical these changes are for our baby. A newborn's adjustment to the world is great, but they have mum or dad to protect them, nurture them, and love them throughout this intense journey.

As mothers, we are finding our way through a distinctly difficult transition as well. We have an abundance of questions, we are in need of reassurance, and we are at the beginning of a drastic change internally and externally which can be unrecognizable, and distorting. This can be the beginning of our loss of self, difficulties in our relationships, a struggle with unrecognizable emotions, our expectations being challenged, and all of those questions pouring out.

Powering through the fourth trimester, focusing on our own personal route into Matrescence, we will be challenged. That challenge can begin our understanding of motherhood. Most importantly, this period of emotional and psychological transition does not always begin as your baby is born. It may filter in at any stage of motherhood.

During this period of change, we will:

- Experience mixed feelings about the changes occurring in our lives.

- Navigate our understanding and expectations of motherhood.

- Challenge our understanding of what being a good mother means to us.

- Confront our past and our attitudes towards parenting.

- Learn an incredible amount about what we can tolerate, manage, juggle, and appreciate.

- Re-evaluate what we know about ourselves.

This transformation has a way of creating a blank slate while also delivering us to a time in our lives that is like a puzzle made up of our experiences, our connections, our beliefs, and so much more. A complex puzzle, with many broken and missing pieces, but one which we can call our own and change if necessary.

It may also feel as though it is something that happens *to* us, but because of the free-thinking people we are, we can question it. We can examine everything in order to understand what part this plays in our lives and our personalities. And we can protect ourselves, comfort ourselves, and be our own guide on this transformational journey.

It is an incredible upheaval within our minds let alone our bodies which take the brunt of physical change after babies are born. When we recognize the importance of this process, we can allow the time and space for it. To unravel this distinctly neurological experience we need to guide ourselves through the transformation by mothering our minds and bodies.

The following are ways in which we can unravel Matrescence from the beginning, as soon as baby is born, but these are important elements to remember at any stage of motherhood.

The Practicalities of Unraveling Matrescence

Build a Lifeline

We were never supposed to do this alone. After the baby, comes the placenta and somewhere in between the pushing, pulling, and shoving, a wondrous self-doubt and anxiety may be birthed along the way too, appearing when you least expect it. It has a glorious way of silently creeping in the door and kicking you in the shins when you think you've finally figured out this new gig. Raising children does not mean you have to have it all figured out at once.

Parenting can be quite the solitary experience, and we can lay a disparaging foundation when we believe we are failing, or not measuring up to our parenting standards. We may not know how to ask for help, or what questions to ask as our expectations are not met, and our adjustment to mothering can be negatively affected. Gaining knowledge from others can help to form realistic expectations and help us to better adapt.[7] Build a lifeline with friends, family, even strangers online, and speak honestly about your experience at any stage of motherhood. This closeness and integrity will get you through many hard days when you realize you are not the only one finding it difficult and are in need of support. The aim with your lifeline is to take motherhood out of the perceived box and rant and rave about her until the rawness is natural and acceptable and you are reminded that you are learning, you are good enough, and you are transforming.

Sleep Like a Baby

The connection between sleep and mental health is not fully understood yet, but studies so far suggest that for positive mental health and substantial emotional resilience, a good night's sleep is beneficial.[8] Chronic exhaustion can set us up for negative thinking, emotional vulnerability, and a poor mental state which can lead to depression.

Positive sleep habits begin during the day. Overtiring ourselves and our children, forgetting to connect emotionally, being overwhelmed, and not going to bed on time, builds our day in a way that night-time becomes a battle. So, ensure you rest well during the day especially when night-time sleep can be a chore with a newborn, or preschooler with an inherently bad sleeping pattern. Take naps, ask for help and rest your mind and body. Forgive yourself, banish guilt, and allow the kitchen sink to overflow. As difficult as that can be, I know! I love a tidy kitchen myself and once mistakenly believed a form of my self-care was maintaining a tidy home. It's not! Recognize the exhaustive state you are living in as your mind and body delineates so much and give yourself the time to rest.

Embrace Yourself

Focusing on the emotional labor of the ebb and flow of this new maternal life, we may often feel overwhelmed by all it entails, forgetting to focus on ourselves. As this transformation takes hold, self-care has never been more important. Yes, our primary responsibility is our children, but remember what they say, "You can't pour from an empty cup" and if you forget to fill your own cup, what do you have to give your children?

Take note of your own needs and make them a priority. Your needs are balanced the same as everyone else's. We require a social connection outside of our children, intellectually stimulating conversation outside of the baby babble, emotional connection with our partner and physical stimulus such as exercise or indulging in our favorite hobby. The experiences pre-motherhood which gave you the rest and pleasure that you actively sought out are more important now than ever. Embrace yourself and give in to indulging in your own needs.

Mind Your Mind

The hormonal shift associated with pregnancy and the postpartum period can affect us all in different ways with one in five of us experiencing a mental health issue either during pregnancy or within the first year of birth. This figure is frighteningly high considering many women are not adequately assessed for mental health problems.

The symptoms of Baby Blues which may occur in the first fourteen days after delivery are considered relatively mild which I contest as I remember heartbreakingly crying for 14 hours straight after the birth of Allegra, alone in a hospital room with a baby who cried equally hard. Baby blues often present with irritability, loneliness, worry, mood swings and restlessness. The Baby Blues will pass however as the rush of hormones in our body begin to regulate.

If your symptoms are stronger than mood changes, including unsettling thought patterns, excessive low mood, and anxiety, then postnatal depression may be the cause. Up to 15% of women experience postnatal depression. It is important if these feelings creep in that you speak to someone who will help. Early intervention is necessary to ensure it does not last longer than it needs to. Your GP, midwife, or public health nurse will advise on how to manage postnatal depression.

Allow Time to Heal

A self-sacrificing nature is somehow added to our personalities when we become mothers. Working through the pain, putting everyone else's needs before ours, and ticking off the never-ending to-do list. Carrying on in such a way will never give us the appropriate time to heal, grow, and learn. Allow yourself the time to heal and don't put pressure on yourself to physically be the woman you were before pregnancy.

The Psychologies of Unraveling Matrescence

Time of Uncertainty

There is this idea that when we have a baby who we have longed for, we should be complete, fulfilled, and joyous. We have spent the past nine months talking to them as they grew in our belly, measuring them in fruit sizes and dreaming about what color their eyes would be. And while we may be enamored by our newborn, we may also crave space, and quiet, and to run from our responsibilities.

Motherhood creates a unique ambivalence which can make us somewhat uncomfortable. We expect to be happy and overjoyed, but we don't expect to feel a sadness or a loss. There is a significant tug of war with our emotions as we learn to balance and accept this ambivalence. Be gentle with yourself as you learn to be mindful of these emotions, of which each and every one is valid.

Embrace Change

This entire period of transformation is riddled with change. From how we think, what we eat, our periods, to how our body looks and even down to the matter of how our day pans out, the change is huge. Fighting against this change, and drastically looking to regain the life before baby will make this transition harder. Everything is changing which is naturally an upsetting occurrence. Embrace this change by remaining open minded as to what your body and mind needs at this crucial crossroads in your life.

Protect Your Relationships

Families are born quite literally out of the intimate connections we have. These connections require due care when our world is rocked by the demanding needs of someone entirely dependent on you. The stress and strain of raising a family can add untold pressure onto a family dynamic. We are left with less energy, time, and attention to give to the equally important relationships in our lives.

Tackle parenthood as a team to avoid resentment or rejection taking over. Support each other in a way that you both feel appreciated, loved, and respected.

The Duality of Motherhood

As we finish up this chapter exploring the idea of motherhood in an attempt to understand the intense transformation which occurs, and begin to question who we are, I cannot ignore the powerful juxtaposition of motherhood. It is something we need to continually remind ourselves of as we carry on this discussion and unravel ourselves. There is an unreasonable duality of motherhood that will always be present. A constant tug and pull of our emotions.

On the one side we are more in love than ever with a little human we barely know, or possibly not yet. We don't know this little person as such. There is instinctual love but possibly not that hearty love of truly knowing someone. That kind of love comes with time. On the other hand, we desperately want time alone, to be free even momentarily from the responsibilities. However, there is some sort of guilt or shame lingering when we lean too far away from that which we believe needs us most, our children.

This duality creates a habit of questioning everything we do. We question our desire to work, and our need to be at home with them and be their primary carer, and the pull to do both, knowing it can be somewhat tricky. We try to balance the belief we should be doing one thing with the kids, only to then feel as though we should simultaneously be managing the house somehow.

We lose as much as we gain in motherhood, which is confusing, disappointing, and sometimes a shock. Our hobbies may be put on hold, our social calendar a lot lighter, our desire to connect with others temporarily waning, and our usual routines disappear overnight. At the same time, we gain a new appreciation for our time, our close ones, and happily watch our newborn grow. These gains and losses send us on an emotional rollercoaster with some incredible lows and daring highs. Recognize these emotions and appreciate each and every one of them.

As you unravel the clichés, remember, we do not need to understand everything right now. We are learning about ourselves, about what we need as women and mothers, and how to incorporate these changes and needs within our life as we raise our children. I will end this section and chapter by reinforcing the message that we are allowed to feel sad for our losses and battle them against our gains. We are allowed to mourn our old life and celebrate the new, all within the same minute.

chapter 2

Unraveling Identity

● **Identity** \ ī-'den-tə-tē \
The distinguishing character or personality of an individual
Dictionary, **Merriam-Webster**

SITTING ON MY TWO-YEAR old's bedroom floor, in darkness, gentle nursery rhymes whistling through the air, I would wait for her to fall asleep before creeping out of the room, dodging the creaking floorboards, and hoping my knees wouldn't groan. Night after night, the same music played as the theme to my early motherhood, and the gentle pats on her back soothed her overtired body. "Lie down, sweetie," pat, pat, pat on repeat as she threw soother after soother out of the cot, and I unconsciously popped them back in as tiredness enveloped me and I fell into the pattern of mothering over being.

The routine, the parental tedium, the duty, and the distinct inability to truly interrupt and slow my thoughts to allow them to flow in a manner I could interpret, seemed never ending. In those first few years of motherhood, I felt invisible as I blurred into the walls. I kept the automatic rhythm of the house whistling, so that all was well, and the kids were looked after.

Everyone and everything were thriving but me.

My love for my kids has never been in question and I will constantly search for ideas to ensure we create ever-lasting memories together. I will do everything in my power to protect, care, and nurture our girls to grow into responsible and independent women. They are my number one priority. However, this conversation is not about our commitment to our children. I have every confidence you are, as much as I am, a wonderful, caring mother who happens to have recognized that she is in a transparent state of flux searching for that missing piece in all of this wonderful endlessness of parenthood.

I am sure there are days you simply adore and others, less so, and moments when you question your choices, abilities, or thoughts. But—there's always a "but" in a conversation which tries to balance the narrative of dedicated love and respect alongside the want and need to run away at times—we need to have room for ourselves in this plotline of motherhood. Space for our minds to breathe in unison with the thoughts in our head. Room to ask questions and find answers. Especially the questions we believe we're not supposed to ask or think about, such as, "Why don't I like my baby yet?" or "Why is Megan so much better at this than me?"

In all of the chaos and long days of mothering, we need time to unravel who we are and who we are becoming because there is an unde-fined loss connected with all of the gain of becoming a mother.

The loss of a lifestyle we became accustomed to. For me, it was the sudden disappearance of impromptu weekend long Star Trek binges or spontaneous getaways to Berlin. We misplace the things that make us tick like our hobbies, our dreams, our desires. Gone was my little homemade jewelry hobby which wasn't the worst little earner on Etsy for a time. And there is a loss of a future that seems stifled because of responsibilities, blocks, and a devastatingly loss of time. I dreamed of being a writer but felt so far removed from its possibility when babies limited my time and creativity.

Now, you can imagine this conversation is prefaced by how our identity is not intrinsically linked to our children, or to our motherhood despite it feeling as though it takes over. Our capabilities are not fundamentally blocked and will not disintegrate because the hand of motherhood tapped us on the shoulder with her long finger. I say this because I am now a professional writer, and it was my motherhood that was the catalyst which sparked this dream into a reality, but it did not simply happen as a result of adding motherhood to my resume but rather because I unknotted that large question of "Who am I?"

It was after the birth of Allegra that I took to blogging, and when Devin came along, I quit that permanent, pensionable, long-term job as a librarian to create a professional career as a journalist and editor (and work from home under the overbearing soundtrack of "Blippi", I might add).

I feel wholeheartedly that being a mum is not what necessarily makes my core beat, but rather it cushions my ability to enthusiastically be the person I have always wanted to be, because—and this is the crux of my personal unraveling—if I were not a mother, I would not be the writer I am. If I were not a mother, I would not be the person I am.

Motherhood created a change, not only in circumstance but also in mind, for me. How I see myself is quite honestly directly affected by the fact that I am a mother of two girls and very proud of that fact. You see, there are changes afoot in all our lives when we are struck by strong transformations. Change creates a catapult. But whether you allow yourself to be propelled or not, is up to you.

Before there are changes there are indeed losses. Losses we must learn to navigate, accept, and move on from if we are to morph our identity with our motherhood. All of our losses are uniquely personal and individual to each of us, meaning my unraveling will likely not match up to yours nor yours to mine.

What is Identity Anyway?

It is easy to feel defined by the world we create as a parent who oversees the domestic duties. We become bound by the routine of other people's lives because it takes time to pull ourselves away from the belief that the routine of the children is greater than any need of the parent. No one will see you or appreciate you unless you let yourself be seen.

Taking ourselves out of the shadows of our kids and illuminating ourselves in all our unknown glory is empowering. It can also be fairly terrifying considering we have to figure out who we are all over again, pulling at the loose threads of our past and stitching them together with the present.

Our identity includes external factors which we ultimately have no control over. Our height, our socioeconomic class, and our race. It includes our political and religious beliefs, our values, and moral attitudes. It is structured by our relationships, our past experiences, our gender, and sexual preferences. There is not one thing that makes us who we are but rather a plethora of considerations, some of which we may not even be aware of.

Our identity develops, changes, and fluctuates depending on our values, our experiences, our past, and our interactions with others. It is not stable and evolves as a result of life changing events.[1] This is something we need to consider when it comes to this transformation to motherhood.

Ordinarily, our identity may unconsciously evolve, be maintained, or strengthen throughout a stable personal environment. However, when a stark transition such as motherhood or divorce effectively overturns what we know, we become more aware of our identity.[2] Yet, we may also be unprepared for or unaware of the intense morphing and revolution of such transformations, and so, it comes as a surprise to us.

The sudden awareness of the change is what my friend referred to as a "culture shock" as we sat opposite each other with squirming babies in our arms. Our babies were born ten days apart and we made a conscious effort to meet for decaf coffee, pecan pie, and social interaction for our drooling babies who were quite frankly more interested in each other's toys and the liquidated rusks. At the time, she was the only mother I knew who explicitly and openly referred to the intensity of motherhood in the same manner as I had, but she managed to phrase it in a way that is so poetically and poignantly stark. A culture shock of epic proportions.

It is a change so vitally embedded in our ethos and values which inherently jolts us unknowingly. This spark, if we don't recognize it, can thrust us in a direction we are not ready for. Our babies were a few months old when we talked about this transformation, and I could see her acceptance of this dynamic change so early on in her motherhood. While she battled with it as much as we all do, she seemed to lean towards it which helped her navigate the transformation a little easier. This culture shock is the catalyst for defining our sense of self.

The Authentic Self

How we experience this transition of accepting, morphing, altering, or regaining our identity can lead us to our authentic self, considering life is, after, all a process with an ever-evolving identity. If it were a fixed entity, we would not try so hard to find ourselves amongst the chaos. German philosopher Martin Heidegger believed "through our reflections of our interactions with others we become aware of ourselves."[3] In some ways, this leads us to question if we are looking to validate our identity through others? When we transition to motherhood are we connecting our root identity to our children, to our job, our colleagues, or are we searching for our actual self, outside of all these elements?

Finding our authentic self during motherhood can become obscured by how we perceive the experience.[4] We may not feel like a mother. This was exactly my experience when Allegra was born. I believed motherhood would simply come to me. I thought I would wake up and feel empowered with a baby, but I did not feel that inward tug on my heartstrings, or that explosion in my mind telling me that I was made for motherhood. My friends and family all seemed to know what they were doing with my little bundle, so I would let them have her. When they left and the door closed, it was just me and the baby. I felt so detached from being her mother. Motherhood was not what I expected and there seemed to be no change in sight. I could barely relate to any aspect of life with babies and yearned after what was now my previous life.

On the other hand, we may adopt a motherhood identity and how we see ourselves may evolve and change. Many of us recognize that there will be some sort of change with a potential identity crisis on the cards when we become mothers. It is after all one of the hot topics at the baby shower along with the amazing cupcakes Hannah brought. We may not realize that birthing a child may mean a complete exodus of the identity we knew and loved and a complete rebuild from the ground up. The problem with losing our identity in such a naked way is that our sense of self and sense of value gets lost. How can we regain any part of ourselves after such a big change? This kind of loss can be palpitating, so we latch on to the idea of motherhood as it inherently becomes a focal point to add some sense of self, whether we believe it or not. It may take a while, but the motherhood identity is fierce.

For many of us, motherhood becomes the "other." A new experience incorporated into our lives to blend with our work identity and home identity. We battle against the addition of the motherhood identity because it is a time of extreme stress and chaotic upheaval. So much so, we create a new character for ourselves by building a narrative which may not necessarily equate to who we are. And so, we continue to unravel.

Then again, some may not feel any different. The mothers who hold on to their sense of self and adhere their focus to themselves but also attach to the understanding that their children are their purpose in life. While they do not feel different, they recognize the importance of the job.

Unravel

How do you perceive your motherhood identity?

☐ I do not feel like a mother

☐ I have adopted a motherhood identity

☐ I do not feel any different

Was this your initial thought?

_____

_____

How do you feel about including motherhood to your identity?

_____

_____

What are the sensations connected with this feeling?

_____

_____

Expanding On Our Sense of Self

For much of my life, my sense of self was such an abstract thought that I didn't give it much time. I was who I was and that was it, but if I took away my family, my identity would be stripped as my experiences with these people over decades has curated, without intention, the person I am. My parents who encouraged me with my writing even at 14 years old when I would come into their bedroom at 11:30pm as they were drifting off to sleep to read them a new obscure 24 line poem about old age that I had written while listening to late night radio; my sister who is seven years older than me and will forever be my best friend as our relationship shifted to true empathy and understanding as I moved into motherhood a few years after her; and my brother who introduced me to my future husband, quite an important aspect of my life if I do say so.

If I took away the three years at university which I hated and avoided to the best of my ability, I would not have a Degree in English and Greek and Roman Civilization, meaning, my career would not have moved into librarianship. If I took away those thirteen years of working in medical and nursing libraries, I would not have the skills to research and write and would not have moved into freelance journalism focusing on family and health.

And then of course there is Barry, my other half who has been by my side since I was 17, my husband since we were both in our early twenties, and who held my hand when our first and second children were born. The untold changes these three additions to my family have had on me sparks an enormous transition in my identity.

But has it been my authentic and real self all these years?

We have discussed this transition and whether the motherhood identity matches our ideals and expectations. A lot of the time it doesn't which means we fail to consider how accepting motherhood and being compassionate with ourselves creates the opportunity to allow the qualities of motherhood to expand within us. Re-evaluating our sense of self asks us to question where motherhood sits in our lives, considering it is personally extensive, affects how we navigate our relationships with more empathy, and is vocationally generous as motherhood enhances our ability to work better.[5]

We have the opportunity to grow our sense of self with motherhood when we reframe our attitudes to this change and unravel the role we play within our family.

Unravel

What choices and actions in your life have led you to this point?

_____

_____

Do these choices bring you closer to your authentic self?

_____

_____

How are you moving towards your true self?

_____

_____

The Great Loss

The losses associated with this stage of our life are fundamentally obscured because we may struggle to look passed the loss or the grief to a time when a flux or change may once again occur, relieving the agony of the current loss. We become blocked with an angst which has yet to be reframed, storing the loss in our bodies, and locking it away.

Add to that the fact that we are exhausted, overwhelmed, and touched out with sensory overload from the persistent and increased noise level in our once quiet homes. We have no head space to unravel these losses, so they grow and become overbearing, obscuring our idea about who we are. Our identity becomes confused as a result.

As I wore out that spot on the carpet, shushing my babies to sleep, my mind switched into survival mode. I felt loss so great I could hardly identify it. Throw in the suspected rules of society and the weight of the patriarchy, and I believed this was how it was for everyone.

I asked questions, but didn't hear answers because, firstly, it was rare for anyone in my circle to feel comfortable in being raw, honest, and open about motherhood, and secondly, because no one else can answer these internal monologues. I was too afraid to listen to myself. I was angry. I was raw, and utterly confused.

My thoughts were negative, and I didn't particularly have a kind word to say about myself or how I managed my motherhood after it rocked up, took over, and told me to sit in the corner like a good little girl.

Over the years I have routinely asked:

- What the hell is actually happening?
- What am I missing?
- Why does it even matter?
- What is wrong with me?

- Why can't I do this?
- Why do I feel unmotherly, unmotivated, and disconnected?

The answers were simple, but I wasn't unraveling deep enough to make sense of it. Of course, motherhood was the thing what was happening, a transformation, a flux, a possible identity crisis. I was missing the woman I used to be, and I most certainly did (and do) matter. Nothing was wrong with me. I was simply adjusting and relearning but did not recognize this. Naturally, I could do this, hell, I was doing this, just not in a way I felt I could embrace.

There is usually a million underlying twisting and turning answers underneath our questions. The answers are not straightforward especially when motherhood is more immense than we ever imagined. The answers are not forthcoming in quick succession like lightning bolt self-awareness. Finding the answers is a slow process of unraveling.

Before I found any tangible answers, as we do in this constant momentum of motherhood, I carried on. Duty. Obligation. Responsibility. It felt as though no one, including me, seemed to notice that I was mid-transformation and panicking about how upended my life and the house was. Like an effervescent ghost guilefully directing our lives through the hours until sundown, I felt unnoticeable, to the world, even to myself when I looked in the mirror. I wanted to connect my journey of motherhood to the person I was or wanted to be. I needed to blend my new and old personalities as one but couldn't find the right size needles to knit them both together, and this made the loss so much greater because it felt irreversible.

The loss was suffocated by doubts and guilt because I wasn't enjoying motherhood as I assumed I should have been. I felt uncomfortable in my body, I missed my lie ins, I hated playtime and had no imagination for My Little Pony stories. I missed holding Barry's hand on a long walk by the coast in lieu of pushing a pram. I lost all my hobbies. I barely listened to music anymore. I longed to travel and to feel confident again, and I hated that no one asked how I was once the baby came. I stopped wearing jewelry unless it was a teething necklace, and I missed being worry free.

My experience of blurring into the background of this invisible job is not unique, but it is also not an expectation of motherhood we must commit to either. Losing our identity is a common narrative around motherhood, told in hyper-negativity as though there is no going back. That's it. We're lost. The kids have done their job. I'm all theirs now. It can feel like this on certain days especially when the mental load ticks over and we are constantly thinking about the kid's bowel movements or checking for lice. However, that's somewhat of a defeatist attitude, as though we cannot be the woman we want to be or pursue our dreams and passions because motherhood comes first, and we must sacrifice all to the queen. No. Simply, no.

Motherhood creates as much as she spits out. We may not choose what stays or goes, but we can evaluate, recreate, and challenge ourselves. She may stir the pot, and possibly dish out potentially undercooked or raw beliefs and understandings of how this recipe of motherhood is meant to look and taste. We may eat it because that's what we think we should do, but another cook, who adds a little extra seasoning and cooking time, can figure out that this change is a good thing, a necessary thing, and a potentially life changing, revolutionary transformation. Motherhood needs us to keep a side-eye on the recipe while keeping the pot from boiling over.

My analogies remind me of a moment when Allegra was four years old. I stood at the cooker; a hot pot of chili thickening as I stirred. She crept up behind me to hug me and as I paused, spoon in hand, her little arms tightened around my waist. My other hand draped across her shoulders and as I gently squeezed back, leaning down to kiss her wispy hair which I forgot to brush that day, some chili slid down the wooden spoon and stung my hand. Not flinching, I felt her tiny hands on my postpartum belly, and all I could think as she hugged me was, "I needed that," quickly followed by the thought, "Shit, I'm mum." It was a moment of internal realization of an identity that had not hit me when she was born, or when she started preschool, or every time I bathed her, or even when her sister was born, but rather when she needed a hug from her mum and the dinner scalded my hand. In the same instant, I also realized that I had so much more mothering to do and that I desperately wanted to do it.

I like to think this was a turning point in my career as mother, and in some ways this acceptance was tied into the internal pivot that happened around the same time as I was crushed under the weight of postnatal depression and anxiety. Nevertheless, these moments of explicit thoughts are there for a reason. They are momentary glimpses of accepting motherhood in its rawness and acknowledging the parental challenges that can pick and chew at our values, expose our vulnerabilities, identify our inadequacies, champion our abilities, and give ourselves permission to fail or soar.

These special moments encourage us to accept our limits but also reach for the stars, focus on how we approach our thoughts and feelings, and persuade us to change our own narrative, piece by piece. It is the compassion, and acceptance, and empowerment we can deliver to ourselves which will shift how we perceive this role.

The Consciousness of Mothering

So much of what we do as mothers occurs naturally, deliberately and without thought. A hidden workload that seems to simply happen. We appear to accept it and move with it. Perfectly ironed shirts magically appear in the wardrobe, the bowls are licked clean with a scrubbing brush, bedsheets are miraculously washed, and the fine layer of dust vanishes before anyone notices it. Tantrums are eased with a hug, sore knees are covered with dinosaur plasters, nightmares no longer linger, and there are always teabags or coffee in the jar for a well-needed brew. We are the multi-tasking parent doing what we do best and knowing what our children need before they even know it themselves. It seems to be organic, expected, just what needs to be done to keep the heartbeat of the house thumping along.

This unprompted consciousness is tied to those ideologies we spoke of; the myths and beliefs and the old adage that says women are the homemakers and will do it all. When we talk about the process of motherhood and the distinct transition, we do not assume that we will become consumed by this responsive nature, but most of us are as the invisible job is a heavily gender imbalanced construct.

Paula Fyans deeply discusses this in her book of the same name, *The Invisible Job: how sharing home and parental responsibilities leads to happier lives*. She says, "The process through which women acquire this invisible job is based on beliefs so ingrained in our conditioning that many women don't even realize it is happening."[6]

Being devoured by this ideology of motherhood shifts our identity and, at the very least, we become lost in the chore of it all. But this is the 21st century and women are choosing, the gender imbalance is shifting albeit painfully slowly, and our experiences are expanding outside of one purpose or a sparse identity.

I barely noticed this change in those first few years as the ordinary days blurred together and the expectations bloated. The dinners were made, lunches prepared, the mess cleared away, toys rotated, and toilets cleaned. A perpetual motion until the loving pat, pat, pat at bedtime. I believed I had some semblance of control which was one of the reasons I sat at the cot and waited until little eyes closed and slept, as though I had some intrinsic part in their naturally falling asleep.

That two-year-old Allegra is now much older and for a few years I replaced her floor with her sister's, and I sat at the same cot, different room, night after night, soothing a new person to sleep. The routine the same. Now, most nights there are stories read, kisses on foreheads, and lights turned out, giving me time and space and drive to refocus my energies back to me. Yet, as I ping the dishwasher on at midnight, I wonder even today do I still feel invisible?

It was those first years, those early days of babies, toddlers, and growing pains when we are duly dismantled as motherhood re-creates aspects of our identity, that I was too exhausted to explore and too busy to recognize that parts of me were slipping away, and that the mental load was becoming unbearably heavy. We're often unaware before the baby arrives that such a change would be so explicit, so unparalleled, so naked.

There is rarely a thank you for the 754 tasks we complete in a day. There is no glory for the three different dinners we make to appease the changing tastes of adults, child, and toddler. There is no applause for the smiles throughout the day or the happy faces that fall asleep after a busy day of making cupcakes, painting, and gluing purple and pink pom poms onto home-made cards. Throughout these early years of parenthood, we are not looking for gratitude, however, but rather some sort of acknowledgement that we are here. We wish to be seen, recognized, allowed the time and space to evolve through this transition, and to find ourselves at the bottom of the toy basket.

I can't deny that I blurred into the life of my kids. I felt that pull of being a mother and almost nothing else beyond that. In some ways I became invisible because I yielded to the natural instincts of being their mother and forgot that I was here too, neglecting to care for myself.

Whatever identity I had was consumed by the motherhood role, the invisible job, and I was not listening to the conversation which played out in my head. The person I wanted to be was intrinsically out of focus. There was no parallel between being me and being mum. I didn't know I could step outside of the motherhood box and if I so dared, not fully re-enter.

Unravel

Before we kick start this rocky pilgrimage to our sense of self, I would like you to indulge in an exercise which opened my eyes to how strong we are as mothers, and how much we do daily, from the emotional care, the physical care, to the playful side of our everyday lives. Lists are the best way to help organize our thoughts when life seems to spiral. They give context, help collect our thoughts, and coordinate our life. This list, however, is not about planning or meeting goals but reflecting on how wickedly amazing you are. Take out your journal. Sit somewhere quiet and comfortably, preferably alone so you have no disruptions because the second list will be long.

List one: Begin by writing down the things you wanted to achieve today. The items which were on your mental to do list. This list may not be that long. When you have written down the items you expected to do. Tick off the things you accomplished, which may be none. Now move on to list two.

List two: Begin by writing down the first thing you did this morning. Then write down the next thing you did, and the next, and so on until the moment you sat down with your journal. As I said this list is long. Stop writing when you feel the list is long enough, when you understand what I'm asking of you.

Take note and reflect on every single task you did from making the beds, getting dressed, making breakfast, emptying the bin, washing your teeth, dressing the kids, brushing their hair, throwing the empty loo roll in the bin, a flow yoga session, a coffee with your best friend, feeding the dog, rebuilding a Lego house, running for the bus, every single solitary task at the office. For as long as you like, continue to write down every task you accomplished throughout the day. The invisible job. The career. And hopefully, what you did explicitly for you.

Reflect: Look at your list and see how much you do in a single day. You are pretty amazing.

Recognizing this incredible list of things you do in that effortless way is not meant to exhaust us but rather highlight how necessary and important we are, how accomplished we are, and how we do so much more in one day than we ever imagine.

It may also highlight just how much or how little we do for ourselves. Compassion for ourselves as women, and not simply as mothers, is a massive part of this unraveling.

I do this list exercise every so often. It both enlightens and angers me. So much so, that one Sunday morning as both the girls and my other half were all glued to the TV, I cried odd bubbling tears as I washed out the bathrooms, straightened out the beds, and tidied the kitchen without any of them looking up from their screens to see what I was up to. I called a family meeting and handed out lists of chores for each of them because I was so overburdened by a job that was not explicitly mine. "I am not the only one living here and messing up this house," I told them, their sheepish faces and furrowed brows looking at me as though I was about to brandish aprons and caps and work them to the bone for twelve hours straight. Their weekly chores have altered my "list" and while I still do the lion's share of housework, I do it knowing I am not the only one conscious of the dust and dirt.

What remains for me is the mental burden, however. Knowing where the birth certs are, when the parent-teacher meeting is, booking the dental check-ups, remembering that the dishwasher needs rinse aid or the bedside clock needs a new battery. The mental burden of motherhood is a significant factor as we ruminate on our identity and navigate the loss of our life before the indeterminate responsibility of being a mother overburdens our lives.

Stepping Outside of the Box

I wanted to be seen for all of who I was and not for simply being mum. I still do most of the 754 tasks required of me in a day. I still chase after the kids. I still make separate dinners, but I have learned to place a value on myself and recognize that in the bedlam of this I am important, and I know I'm needed. Most importantly, I know I am not invisible.

While my kids are old enough to soothe themselves to sleep now, I still find myself on occasion sitting on the floor again, cramping my legs for the millionth time, gently shushing an overtired little one to sleep. However, now I silently and gently applaud myself for the things I have done through-out the day, making myself visible to me. I tell myself I am important, I matter, and I am pretty amazing for all the shit I get done in a day. This is just the beginning. Acknowledging my workload before separating myself from that workload because again, we are not defined by motherhood, the invisible job, or the mental load which often comes with that.

When all the elements of our "self" come into play, we are left to question everything including:

- Our body
- Our relationships

- Our career
- If we are bonding or not with the baby
- Whether we are giving each of our children enough individual time and attention
- Where we sit in society
- And so much more

We talk about the change so irreverently in mother and baby groups, or over coffee with our friends, without really grasping the reality of this transformation. It. Is. Huge. And almost impossible to comprehend unless we are actively living it.

The consciousness of motherhood is but one element that has a tiring impact on our sense of self. The patriarchy is another. The lack of a name and being called "Allegra's mum" instead of Geraldine is a step further. The inability to find the time to care for yourself despite being overwhelmed and exhausted adds to the influence. In the end, your life becomes completely consumed by the motherload.

Finding our sense of self begins with stepping outside of the box we have fallen into (and not through our own fault). For me it took postnatal depression to unravel my identity, to find my place and understand where I wanted to be. It took postnatal anxiety for me to realize that I did not want to be defined by my mental health or my motherhood. And it took strength and courage to deeply connect with myself and become self-aware.

If we want someone, anyone, to be conscious of who we are, beyond the four walls of our house, beyond the title of mum, we can start by seeing and appreciating ourselves first. We become conscious of ourselves by understanding who we are, who we became, and most importantly who we want to be, by placing a value on ourselves.

Ask yourself:

- Are you invisible to yourself? Do you recognize everything you do? Do you acknowledge your workload, your compassion, your empathy for others?

- Do you share the load, both the physical and the mental, with someone else or are you left to do everything? How can you change this?

- Have you told anyone how you feel about being invisible or being left to do everything without anyone noticing your pain, tiredness, or overwhelm?

Our identity is a diverging path made up of our experiences, our interactions with others, and our translation of all these events. Not by ticking a box, and not by defining ourselves by societies standards. We have choices to make, experiences to explore, and thoughts to ponder. Our actions are a culmination of us as a whole. And so, I am telling you we can own our motherhood and not be defined by it if we have the ability to break ourselves out of the box and unravel our identity.

Unravel

Take some time to consider the following questions. Using your note-book, jot down words, phrases, or even doodles which conjure up ideas and answers to these questions.

- What role do you play within the family?
- Are you happy with that role?
- How can family support you in your familial role?
- Is there anything you don't like about the role you play?
- What is difficult about the role?
- If you could play any role in the family, what would it be and why?

Recognizing Self-Loss

When we feel disconnected from ourselves or question who we are, we may doubt our identity and feel lost in the spectrum of life. We may consume the ideals of others and go along with the status quo, stay attached to unhealthy relationships, say yes when we mean no, and avoid forming our own opinion. This self-loss can leave us feeling:

- **Critical of ourselves.** Doubt, judgement, and negative thought patterns filter their way into our lives.

- **Lost.** Questioning who we are, our role in life, within our family, our job, and our community.

- **Disconnected.** We search for a deep connection with someone or something to replace the loss, or alternatively disconnect or struggle to connect with those closest to us.

- **Impulsive.** Looking for anything that can lead to a sense of gratification or satisfaction. We search for what will give us more meaning, reason, or passion in our lives.

- **Confused.** We question our values, spirituality, beliefs, interests, relationships, and careers.

- **Unfulfilled.** Our sense of self has fragmented.

The self-loss can be triggered by a grief, trauma, or a changing role in our lives. We can either avoid it by creating an illusion of calm or we can question the choices we make every day as we blend with a new identity or an evolving sense of self, accepting these vast changes and making them work for our present and our future.

When we recognize this as a loss, we can decide whether we want to be curious about this change in our lives and choose how to unravel it. Do we go along with it, allow ourselves to be consumed by a new personality which may not align with our values or speak up with the inward retaliation that has us questioning who we are and who we want to be?

These questions will unravel and transform those aspects of your identity that don't quite work for you and help you to embrace those that do. You are here with me after all, unraveling.

Unravel

Take some time to consider the following questions. Using your notebook, jot down words, phrases, or even doodles which conjure up ideas and answers to these questions.

- Is this transition into motherhood having a minimal or significant impact on your identity, personality, daily life? How does this make you feel?
- How can you be kind to yourself as you navigate this transition?
- How can you grow through this change?
- What lessons are you learning as you unravel?

Pulling the Threads of Loss

It's ok to grieve the loss of our identity. It's ok to feel the emotions caused by self-loss. The word grief conjures up ideas of death and black foreboding, but grief encompasses all loss. We can grieve broken relationships, the loss of a job or other livelihood, and we can most certainly grieve the loss of the person we no longer find amidst the spit up on our shoulders and the dark circles under our eyes.

Grieving the loss of a life once lived, of a personality now shadowed, creates space that allows us to feel our emotions surrounding this change, to act on the impulses and feelings we may otherwise suppress or avoid. Every emotion we have is valid. Having the ability to acknowledge how we feel about this loss is important to help us to move on.

We could fight against this grief, believing we should step straight into motherhood because that's what we are supposed to do; be grateful for what we have been given because motherhood is a treasured thing. Which of course it is, but mothering under a grief we don't accept or work through will make this grief spiral and resentment filter into our lives.

Navigating this transformation by acknowledging it as a loss, helps us to identify how we are feeling and connect us with the present, mindfully moving us from the hurt of the loss to the opportunity of the present.

We are ever changing, ever evolving in our journey through life. Motherhood is one hell of a big change and if we are grieving an identity, we should also recognize that this process of grief is not linear, that it may not end in its entirety, and that it is different for every single person.

Unraveling Complex Negotiations

There's a very particular feeling when you run a razor for the first time through your short hair and allow it to gently skim your shoulders as it falls to the ground. Slight panic and intense exhilaration in one second. Holding your breath, silently egging yourself on as you start in the middle where your forehead meets your now naked scalp.

I shaved my head for the first time when I was 34 years old, mid-December, mid-winter, six months after Devin was born and three months after I was diagnosed with postnatal depression and anxiety. I was seeing a counsellor and making progress but also remained crippled with panic and anxiety attacks. Buzzing my head felt in part like retaliation mixed with a rejuvenation as I wandered through maternity leave with a baby and a preschooler.

The identity crisis was palpable, but this was not a break-down but a sharp search for myself. If I could break free from rules momentarily, I could shock myself into finding some part of myself. I struggled to be someone, anyone, as panic and anxiety took hold in those early days of second motherhood. The difference was, despite this being quite possibly the most difficult part of my life thus far, I was not going to sit idly by and allow external forces take control of my life as I did the first time I became a mother.

I sat under ink and needle for hours and tattooed the story of my motherhood on my arm. There, above the veins and bones of my body, sits a wise owl whose eyes are clocks displaying the time of day our children were born, cogs and gears show the ever-fluid motion of life, and a naked woman under moonlight prepares to rise in all her strength and poise.

I reinvented myself but my identity had not changed. On the outside I appeared new, strong, and determined. Inside, I was still stuck. Fragile. Vulnerable. Full of knots.

I spoke with Dr. Janina Scarlet about this concept of unraveling our identity. Janina, a licensed clinical psychologist, and award-winning author of varying titles including *Super-Women: Superhero Therapy for Women Battling Depression, Anxiety and Trauma,* has contributed to a number of pop culture psychology books and unraveled her own thoughts on identity, place, and past lives. A Ukrainian-born refugee, she survived Chernobyl radiation and persecution. At the age of twelve she immigrated to the United States with her family. She later developed *Superhero Therapy* after being inspired by the X-Men.

"Some people might think of it as our identity," Janina tells me. "Some might refer to it as our internal compass, while others might refer to it as our core values. Regardless of the term, acknowledging it might allow us to figure out how to respond to a situation in which a major shift occurs. For example, does our identity, our core values, include being a compassionate person? If so, then it would imply that when we become a parent and when we are stressed out, we can remind ourselves of who we are and what we stand for, to take a breath to care for ourselves, and then show up for our child in a caring and a compassionate way."

It took another two and a half years, therapy, and a lot of writing to unravel my thoughts about who I am, why I exist, and why the self-loss I experienced mattered so much. In the end, I have not regained my identity pre-kids. I have added and added and added—skills, thoughts, practices, dreams, desires—and evolved my identity. Exploring this idea with Janina, she says, "I believe that it is more like redefining our identity and merging it into our existing one. For example, we might have already had the identity of a compassionate human, friend, and partner. Now our identity might be expanded to include being a compassionate human, friend, partner, and parent."

I found it to be a particularly complex negotiation as I gave up parts of myself for something stronger, possibly less flattering. In the end, pulling the threads of motherhood in its elaborate, tangled mess, showed me vibrant threads to work with as I stitched myself back up. In essence, I came to understand that exploring our vulnerabilities and flaws can help us to accept all parts of ourselves and Janina supports this idea. She says, "I think people believe that they have lost their identity when they only focus on the one new aspect of their identity, neglecting others. It might be challenging to balance different parts of ourselves and yet, it might be most beneficial for our well-being. It is important that wherever possible we still engage with other aspects of our identity. For example, if we are an artist, it is important that we still make art, even if it involves doodling for five minutes a day."

Pulling the Threads of Identity

A buzzcut is not the way to find ourselves again, but it serves as an analogy for how we can unravel our identity. Stripping ourselves back to our naked glory so we can truly see ourselves for the first time again. Seeing ourselves this way allows us to unearth where we came from, challenge what we have learnt over the years, especially the time since we became a parent, and identify what truly matters to us.

Janina reminds us that the assumption that we are losing our identity might make us believe that we don't know who we are anymore, and as a result, we might not know how to respond in specific situations. She says, "Sometimes, this "identity crisis" is an indication that we need to step back and take some time, even five or ten minutes to rest, breathe, meditate, perhaps in silence whenever possible, and then consider who we are as a person. Even if we have become a new parent, we are still the same person, as in we are still a kind person, for example. It merely means that there is one more person we are kind toward."

We may be surprised by the answers that come up for us. We may be angry with how much we realize has disappeared. We will most certainly feel a little lighter in answering these questions for ourselves.

Unearthing where we came from: Here we look at understanding our original intentions in life, the values we grew up with, the beliefs we held close, the lessons we have learnt over time.

What were you encouraged to believe?

_____

_____

What mattered the most to you?

_____

_____

What boundaries were in place to protect you?

_____

_____

Challenging what we have learnt over the years: Growing up we may challenge these concepts which have been embedded in our lives for so long. Our choices become more apparent which may conflict with our parents' ideals, or our friends' values. We learn more about ourselves the more inward we look.

Who am I? Who am I really?

_____

_____

What are my true values?

_____

_____

What has happened in my life to shape my values?

_____

_____

What are my passions?

_____

_____

Do my experiences make me who I am?

_____

_____

Identifying what truly matters to us: How we respond to our environment because of our experiences can help us to figure out what we genuinely want to achieve in this world, whether that is personally within our family unit, or in the wider context of the community. Who we are, is a blend of all of our choices.

How can I help others by using my beliefs and values?

_____

_____

What do I want to do, career or otherwise, in the world?

_____

_____

What gets me up in the morning?

_____

_____

Pulling the Threads on Our Origin Story

Unraveling a strong part of my identity has included a lot of what I consider to be soul-searching. It was in many ways unguided and so this part of my unraveling was an obscure untying of threads I struggled to unwind, unknot, or loosen. The threads crossed over, some ripped completely, and others were delicately stitched up only to unravel again. That is until I was introduced to Janina's *Superhero Therapy* which, as a self-professed geek, I was ultimately drawn to.

Whoever our heroes are, be it She-Ra or Harry Potter, there is more to these characters than their power, strength, or the ability to throw a bad guy through a solid brick wall. Often, they are flawed characters with dynamic stories we can relate to on a very human level. For this reason, superheroes are now used in a form of therapy, encouraging us to consider our background and our own origin story which forms our identity, motivation, and internal battles.

Superhero therapy, which incorporates not only traditional superheroes but anything we relate to from pop-culture or fandom, is designed to help promote self-acceptance, self-compassion, and positive behavioral changes which I feel is a perfect fit to include a discussion on here as we unravel our identity. Unearthing my own Origin Story and Superhero Story as I incorporated examples from geek culture into my own understanding, is a process I used to unravel my experience in this transition.

Janina developed *Superhero Therapy* to help her clients become the heroes of their own journey. She explains that the idea of exploring our origin story allows us to view our struggle as the beginning of our heroic path. Our origin story leads to our superhero story.

In her book, *Super-Women,* Janina reminds us that everyone has an origin story, and that most superheroes have a traumatic original story. "In fact," she says, "most heroes' journeys begin with a loss, a trauma, abuse or a lifechanging hurt. It is in facing this pain and growing—not just despite but because of it—that some superheroes are made. Many origin stories are painful, most of them are life changing. It is part of the human experience."[7]

She tells me that an origin story is anything that shifts our lives in another direction. "It is the beginning of a new journey and motherhood certainly is a new journey," she says. "Sometimes even the most wonderful events shift our lives in a different direction and add challenges we never before considered. And as we focus on our sense of purpose, in other words, our core values, we can focus on becoming our own version of a superhero in real life on this new adventure. It is important to remember that superheroes aren't perfect, which means that we don't have to be the 'perfect' parent to be a super-parent. We just have to care enough to show up and do our best."

For my own unraveling, along with the idea of the origin story, I looked to my favorite science fiction film produced in Germany in 1927, *Metropolis*. Since I studied English at college, and explored the complexities of this silent, black and white movie, I have been fascinated with the character of Maria (and subsequently developed a life-long love of robots as an automaton is made in her image to curb a rebellion).

In this pop-culture favorite, both human Maria and robot Maria, played by German actress Brigitte Helm, are characters whose identities are threatened by patriarchal institutions. They are used as pawns to increase the greed of corrupt business and lose themselves in the process. The perseverance and determination of Maria (both human and robot) to rebel against their oppressors and achieve what they desire was a turning point in my understanding of myself. My oppressor was not only my idea of motherhood in line with the clichéd ideals offered to me, but also the wavering mental health that knotted me up.

"The origin story exercise allows us to view our struggle as the beginning of our heroic journey. And it is up to us to decide the rest," says Janina.

Try working through some of the below prompts in pursuit of understanding your origin story:

- How did you get to where you are today?

- Think about something you wish you knew ten years ago. What advice would you give to your past self, and how would your life have changed as a result?

- Finish the sentence: "I got to where I am today because I am _____."

- What are your main coping mechanisms? Are they serving you well?

- Imagine you could do anything you wanted to do without being judged. Would anything change in your life?

- Describe a mistake you made recently. How did you deal with it?

- Finish the sentence: "I need to accept that _____."

- What made you stronger in life?

- What can you do today to prepare yourself for future disappointments?

- Describe an experience that changed you for the better.

- What's going well in your life right now?

- How do you show compassion to others? Can you extend that same kindness to yourself?

- What do you most want your children to learn from you?

- What do you love most about your personality? What qualities do you find hard to accept?

- What difficult thoughts or emotions come up most often for you?

- What parts of daily life cause you stress, frustration, or sadness? What can you do to change those experiences?

- What aspects of your life are you most grateful for?

Write Your Origin Story

Take some time to think about your origin story. As you write, think about the events that have occurred that affected you, and what your reactions have been to those events. Our stories have a strong effect on our present and on how we navigate our lives in the moment. As we unravel our motherhood, we may recognize where events in our past have impacted our present.

The Slow Process of Motherhood

Our identity gets a little warped as we lose an aspect of independence we had worked hard to acquire. Our expectation of who we are and how to blend all of that into a new world of nappies, soothers, and hours in the day which we no longer own, can force this massive change to linger on the side-lines longer. We fight it. We fear it. We hate it and are angry that it seems to be taking so much away from us.

Finding a balance on the duality of motherhood is difficult because we were not really ready to give up so much of ourselves. Not our time, or our bodies, not our minds, our thoughts and love for ourselves. We can hate all of this and love it at the same time. We can feel empty and so perpetually full. We can feel terrifyingly lost and wonderfully found. We can feel like a nobody rather than a somebody, but by flipping this narrative, we can reframe it to make sense of our purpose in life at the present time.

We become so engrossed with this new maternal takeover. So much so that we find ourselves in a fast-paced life with little ones and quite a big to-do or done list, and we tend to put ourselves at the end of that list. Remembering you are someone, that you are you, that you are still in there pounding on your ribcage to get out and explore, takes time. It is a slow process. Parental self-care is a must, but instead, how many of us push ourselves aside for the greater good of the family? How many times has your coffee gone cold? How many times did you get up from your dinner plate to fetch this, that or the other for the kids? How many meals did you even eat today? How long did you pause and stop to check if you were still in there?

If you're like me, chances are, you have had one proper meal and grazed for the rest of the day. You may have picked up some leftover toast, realized the kid already licked the butter off, but ate it anyway. Maybe you left the dinner table eight times for more water, ketchup, a wipe to clean the toddler's hands or something else trivial but necessary to keep the peace. You never even had the chance to put a pot of coffee on and you haven't had a minute's peace to yourself, not even a solo trip to the loo.

Finding five minutes for yourself in a whole twenty-four hours sounds plausible but it is not always possible when your kids are so small. Remembering and taking time to focus on just me during the day, in the evening, on weekends, has helped to reconnect with myself, the real me. I forgive myself for needing and wanting alone time. Time to recollect my thoughts and congratulate myself for getting through another day without letting the pressure of life pull me down, without anxiety or stress building up.

I'm my own cheerleader because if we don't cheer for ourselves, who will? We all have our own drama in life, so give yourself a little cheer in case no one else gets a chance to.

We can own our motherhood. Not only can you be the mother you want to be, but you can fight the challenges and the tough days and make this experience of being mum greater than you ever envisioned. It will challenge you. It will disappoint you. It will be hard and demanding, but you are not solely defined by motherhood if you have the ability to break yourself out of the box.

Although this process is slow, remember our book is unwritten. The pages are crisp, clean, and empty, waiting for you to scribble a few tales and cross a few mountains, shed a few tears, and burst with love and excitement. We are the characters in our own book. The feisty ones. The nervous ones. The ones with an untold story. The ones with secrets. The social ones. The scared ones, and the sacred ones. The fantastical and magical. The ordinary. The new. The adventurer. We are the plotlines that twist and turn, fall, and soar. The stories that plateau, all of a sudden, for an uncomfortable length of time and as quick as everything seems relaxed, a jolt revs the story on.

We are the story we don't want to end. We are the characters we love and feel for. We are the pages magically adorned with words as the seconds tick by. There is no expectation to do more. To do better. To change. To push yourself harder. What you have is worth reading and living.

Hello you. You are someone. Now, tell me, who is that someone?

chapter 3

Unraveling Triggers

Triggering \ tri-g(ə-)riŋ \
to cause an intense and usually negative emotional reaction in (someone)
Dictionary, **Merriam-Webster**

I KNOW I AM NOT ALONE in being routinely triggered by intense parenting moments. At least I know this now. Before, I thought I was the only one wading through a surging storm as the intensity of these overloaded moments threatened to tip me over the edge. The moment doesn't have to be anything too elaborate. With the emotional overwhelm of motherhood, we can simmer along, close to boiling point, for much of the day. Stepping on a random, misplaced Lego piece could be the thing that triggers us to react in an emotionally unbalanced way. The Lego is not the cause but rather a catalyst for underlying emotions and events which we have yet to unknot in our lives.

After school—when the homework comes out, arguments ensue, the dinner goes on, work emails ping from my back pocket, and the TV blares loud from an empty room because the kids are chasing each other through the corridor of our bungalow while my nerves rattle waiting for a collision with a door jamb—tends to be my ultimate trigger point. Everything is loud. The house is too busy, and my to-do list expands from fitting on one post-it note to the size of a broadsheet newspaper. At the core of it, I have lost control, and needing to be in control is a trigger of mine which I continually work at.

Over time, I have learned to unknot my afternoon narrative from one of chaos and crisis to coffee and calm, or at least calmer. Midday is a time I have recognized to be exactly when I am physically and mentally depleted, so the good coffee comes out. Not the instant roast, because the good coffee means I have made that distinct choice and have control over at least my caffeine options. The afternoons are perplexing to say the least, but I have discovered how easily I can be triggered by a loss of control and intense sensory overwhelm.

Leaning into compassion, and the buzzword of the decade, self-care, has helped alleviate my afternoon tension, but I am not immune to being triggered. I am human, and vulnerable, and unraveling as much as any mother who deflates internally wishing she could crawl inside her own space where everything is quiet and less intrusive.

I have been submerged in unblocking the toilet (think down to the elbow in the U-bend) as the toddler shouts from another room that her sister hit her, while the other one retaliates by pinching her tattletale sibling, at the same time as she knocks over a full glass of milk onto the rug. I'm not sure what they thought I could do for them at that moment in time but the more they complained, cried, and directed their frustration at me as I was quite literally stuck in an inflexible position set me off. Yes, they are kids being kids, and this kind of thing happens, repeatedly, in all our households. They are not going out of their way to upset me or light my fuse. My triggers are just that, *my* triggers. And that's ok, but it's also ok to admit that there are times when we do not handle these situations all that well.

Moments can continue to build, as we hold the tension in our minds and bodies, knotting us up more and more. What we have to do is figure out why we react this way, and what we can do about those reactions and automatic responses to certain situations.

The fact that there are plenty of these moments in an otherwise long day is something we can forget as we feel the exploding nature of frustration, anger, and annoyance tick over during a mundane midweek day. We blame, guilt, or shame ourselves for how we reacted to the kid when she knocks an entire pepper canister, by accident, onto her perfectly cooked and uneaten dinner. You can imagine how this scenario may play out with raised voices and scraping of chairs as kitchen paper is haphazardly used to save something of the over seasoned dinner. But I will save you the dramatization because the point is that we can apologize for our behavior and recognize why we reacted in such a strong way, learning how we can respond better the next time (not that there will be a next time, the pepper is off the table).

Parenthood can feel like the ultimate game of guessing, questioning, and becoming increasingly frustrated until—boom—we are irreverently triggered, and everyone stops to look with wide eyes as we explode to whatever parenting problem has sparked the motherload of eruptions. While their little eyes search out why mum reacted so loudly, we internally shrink with emotional and physical exhaustion compounded by guilt for how our overwhelm or trigger exploded out of our chest.

Remember, our moments, our reactions, are not the entire picture of how we mother as a whole but are rather snapshots of our vulnerability as humans. Triggers leave us immediately reacting rather than responding to our kids. The reaction is usually not in keeping with the moment in time and are often triggered by our past, or something unresolved in our minds.

In this chapter, we are looking at unraveling our triggers, navigating our mental capacity, and our vulnerability. It is not the easiest of chapters with no direct answers, but it will bring a deeper understanding of how we respond to life as mum, what blocks are hidden within us, and how we can navigate memories as they resurface.

Motherhood is a beautiful experience when the balance of understanding life, us, and our role as mother weighs in our favor. When the scales need a little reset, it is not a failing on our part to be unable to naturally weigh life. It gives us a chance to recognize and find the tools to maintain a satisfying equilibrium that includes being self-aware of our limitations and experiences. It means recognizing we are human, vulnerable humans, who may end up utterly exposed.

Being honest about how we experience motherhood is frightening because we open ourselves to criticism. We are left challenging what other people think about us and challenging ourselves. So, before we unravel, let me remind you to do what works for you. To breathe. Be honest, kind, and appreciate the rawness of your emotions. Avoid comparison and remember that you are enough.

It would be remiss of me to not discuss at least some elements of our varying and obstructive maternal mental health in this chapter as the idea of triggers also plays heavily with the knots of our mental wellbeing. However, unraveling our mental health completely is far more complex than I can ever discuss here. I urge you to talk to someone and get expert advice in unknotting your mind in motherhood. Pulling the threads on our mental health is a long and winding road towards navigating the inner workings of our mind, and it is best done in the care of a professional.

The Knots of Maternal Mental Health

Looking down at the bundle of blankets I held gently, but awkwardly, in my lap, I felt an implicit rush of euphoria after Devin was born. An instant feeling of being an invincible protector of her tiny world engulfed me. Life held a momentary perfection, and I enjoyed this pause. This was how my motherhood was meant to stay. Those slow days of early motherhood, smelling baby's head as her big sister sat at my feet, drawing a rainbow with the colors in perfect order.

But while this baby, with a head of pale blonde hair, was beautiful and perfect in every way as her tiny hand curled around my finger, I was not.

As wonderful as the memory is of sitting on the hospital bed twelve hours post c-section with a dainty baby lying on my legs as I talked to her, loved her, and practically inhaled her, I was also delivered into the center of postnatal depression and anxiety. Almost as soon as she began growing inside the walls of my body, born with this new motherhood, was postnatal depression and anxiety. An anxiety I continued to battle as she took her first steps and said her first words.

Postnatal depression and anxiety are not something you ever prepare yourself for when reading the parenting books, folding the Babygro's, testing the baby monitor, and decorating the nursery. "It won't happen. Not to me." But the prevalence of maternal mental ill health is higher than we may know. More than one in ten women worldwide experience mental health difficulties during and after pregnancy according to NICE who say that "Depression and anxiety are the most common mental health problems during pregnancy, with around 12% of women experiencing depression and 13% experiencing anxiety at some point; many women will experience both. Depression and anxiety also affect 15-20% of women in the first year after childbirth. During pregnancy and the postnatal period, anxiety disorders, including panic disorder, generalized anxiety disorder (GAD), obsessive-compulsive disorder (OCD), post-traumatic stress disorder (PTSD) and tokophobia (an extreme fear of childbirth), can occur on their own or can coexist with depression."[1]

The change in my personality, my moods, and my behaviors were so stark and explicit that my family recognized I was battling a desperate state of damaged mental health before I could comprehend these feelings and reactions myself. I was triggered by anything and everything that seemed to take me away from that initial euphoric state of happiness. Everything was a danger. Risk was everywhere and I needed to cocoon myself with my newborn to feel safe.

Asking for and finding help took every ounce of courage and confidence at a time when I was heavily drained of both. I received no support or care from my General Practitioner who discarded my experience as being minimal, something I would just get over if I went for a bath or read a book. I was thrown medication without a full discussion or understanding of my situation and became what I felt was a tick-box exercise. I wanted to know what was happening to me before discussing a medicated route. I wanted to support my mind in a way I felt comfortable with, but no-one would talk to me or guide me outside of giving me pills. Not taking medication was my own choice as my experience in that area was subjective and my reactions to medication have had a poor history.

Medication is a valuable support in managing our mental health. This conversation is about finding a way to navigate your mental health that is suitable for you, your lifestyle, and your family. I advocate for strong mental wellbeing by whatever means you need. It is ok to see a counsellor, to take medication, to ask for help, to cry.

It wasn't until the Public Health Nurse sat across from me and my wriggling new-born at a standard check-up that I felt a weight lift, an exposed and naked weight, that was ultimately freeing. She looked me straight in the eye and asked, "And how are you doing Mum?" I had not been asked this question so explicitly and frankly. I couldn't answer. I fell in a heap and cried because she gave me an opening to swell and purge every emotion that was stored in my body as the tears that fell down my cheeks told her I needed help. I was unraveling in a most necessary way. I needed to be held and cared for. It was this encounter which saw the beginning of my recovery as she helped me find the courage to take that step to make that phone call and start counselling.

It takes one question, one firm hold to show an aching mother she is seen, and heard, and loved. The threads of motherhood are so irreverently knotted that there are times when we need someone else to pull on the thread, hold the spool, or read the pattern.

Pulling the Threads on Baby Blues

I cried for twelve hours straight on the second night of my five-night hospital stay after Allegra was born. Visiting hours meant Barry had to leave the hospital and from the corridor of the ward, I watched him wave goodbye to me and our newborn daughter as the elevator doors closed. Before his face disappeared, my lip trembled, and he was gone merely seconds before the palpitating tears started and didn't end until my tea, cereal, and toast were rolled in on a trolley at 9 am the next day.

I didn't sleep that night. Neither did Allegra, who I was convinced hated me and didn't need me as I bottle-fed her after an emergency caesarean section left me not only mourning my planned birth but struggling to move for pain which complicated my breastfeeding journey in those first hours. I already felt as though I had given up on mothering because I couldn't feed her or soothe her. At least, these were the thoughts spiraling through my head at 3 am as I cried hurtful, sorrowful tears less than two days into motherhood. My beginning was not the joyful experience I had assumed it would be.

This was baby blues. About 80% of us will experience an emotional upheaval after giving birth which is mixed with bouts of sadness, anxiety, worry, stress, and mood swings. We do not particularly know what causes them, but we can hazard a guess that the extreme hormonal fluctuations our body undergoes around birth play a particularly large part in it. Our uterus is shrinking back to its normal size, we are lactating, bonding, and exhausted.

Baby blues happens to four out of five of us, up to two weeks after birth, yet it is often pushed aside as being something women must contend with and move on from. It is one of the reasons why I did not ring the bell to ask for help from a nurse or midwife. It is one of the reasons why I did not tell Barry that I spent the night grieving my lack of maternal love.

Symptoms of Baby Blues include:

- Crying or feeling upset over minor triggers like the diaper bag falling onto the floor.

- Feeling irritable or experiencing mood swings such as both loving and hating the nurse who checks your stitches.

- Feeling unattached or unable to bond with your new-born who already knows your smell and voice.

- Feeling worried or anxious about your baby's health, safety, and wellbeing.

- Unable to sleep even though you are exhausted.

- Feeling foggy and unable to think clearly or make decisions.

There is no explicit treatment for baby blues except sleeping and resting as much as you can, asking for help, and being kind and compassionate to yourself. These emotions are normal. They happen to the best of us, and they will pass. In the meantime, care for yourself, eat well, get fresh air, and talk to someone. The benefits of opening up, sharing our burdens and offloading are long lasting, because one conversation can shift and realign our entire path. Through open conversations we learn and curate skills that can help later on in life as we become more reflective, self-compassionate, and open to listening to, understanding, and advocating for our feelings.

Pulling the Threads on Postnatal Depression and Anxiety

Fifteen percent of us will be hit with something more than the baby blues. I was two weeks postpartum on Devin when I realized that I lost my trust in myself. I know how lucky I am to have uncovered this so early in new motherhood. My behavior, attitude, mood, and the overbearing panic attacks were more than simply being overwhelmed with a new-born and a preschooler. I had a difficult pregnancy on Devin with a subchorionic hematoma (a bleed) at ten weeks. The agonizing worry I had during pregnancy that I needed to protect her and effectively hold her in until she was ready to come out, continued after she was born and as such an overly cautious mother was also born.

During Devin's first year, when I supposedly should have been consumed by the new baby smell, the milestones, and the leaps, I was devoured by an incapacity to do anything at all. I avoided making phone calls, barely made it outside, and couldn't decide what to have for dinner. I struggled to make any decision at all, and put things like a boiler service, changing the milk order, and booking dentists appointments on the long finger. I was quick, too quick, to frustration and anger and I experienced thirty plus anxiety or panic attacks in a day.

I was, in many ways, lost, afraid, spiraling out of control, and routinely triggered when my beautiful children did the littlest of things that came naturally to them.

My body reacted to the anxiety with dizzy spells and shaking, nausea, tension, headaches, and breathlessness. This was more than an overwhelming panic at an attempt to juggle family life, keep everyone fed and watered, and ultimately alive. I struggled to understand the sheer whirlwind blowing in my head and stomach, let alone explain it to someone else or ask for help. I felt worthless, guilty, insecure, and powerless. But I learned that I was not alone and reached out to find the support I needed.

Symptoms of Postnatal Depression and anxiety include:

- Crying when you don't know why.
- Being so exhausted and yet still unable to sleep or sleeping too much.
- Eating without having any interest in food.
- Unexplained aches, pains, or illnesses.
- Feeling irritable, anxious, or angry and unable to control those emotions.
- Sudden mood changes and a feeling of being out of control.
- Difficulty remembering things, being unable to concentrate, or make decisions.
- A lack of interest in things you used to enjoy.
- Feeling disconnected from your baby and not understanding why motherhood is not the way you believed it would be.
- Feeling overwhelmed, hopeless, guilty, and worthless.
- Feeling as though you are a bad mother or that your baby doesn't need you.
- Withdrawing from life.
- Intrusive thoughts of hurting yourself or your baby.

The symptoms of postpartum depression and anxiety are much more severe than those of baby blues, can last much longer, and can begin to appear up to a year after birth. Without treatment, these symptoms can become progressively worse.

Treatment for depression comes in two forms: medication and therapy, with an overlap of the two recommended in certain cases. There should be no stigma or shame attached with either treatment option. Ensure you maintain an honest and open conversation about your mental wellbeing with your care provider. It is only through recognizing and understanding where your mental health sits that you can receive the care and attention you need to find your way out of depression to a solid state of empowering mental wellbeing.

Pulling the Threads on Postpartum Rage

The unspoken emotion of motherhood is postpartum rage which falls under the umbrella of postpartum depression. It is not something we talk about all that often as it conjures up images which are heavily stigmatized and shamed. For me, the anxiety was overwhelming and triggered a rage like I had never experienced before. I threw plates and bowls of cereal and watched as the pieces of ceramic and wet food smashed into the sink splashing onto the kitchen window as though it was an out of body experience. I slammed doors and broke glass and hurled my fist against walls. I shouted and screamed incoherently in front of my children, when they were asleep, and as such that desire to scream into the night sky in the neighboring fields was never stronger.

These feelings and actions were terrifying as I lost control and had a distinct inability to calm my mind or control myself. It was much more than the standard frustration of family and work life. There was a genuine fear about what these actions meant and how far they would go. As such, it was something I never admitted to in my years of sharing my postnatal depression and anxiety journey on social media or through my journalism. I felt ashamed, hurt, and scared. If I admitted to what I was experiencing I believed I would be judged, my children taken from me, and Barry would hate me and leave me. Rage was not a conversation you had over coffee with a friend.

There is no official diagnosis of postpartum rage or anger, and yet, being triggered into rage postpartum or at random stages of motherhood is common. Feminine rage, in our patriarchal world, is heavily knotted with shame, fear, and stigma. Anger is not associated with being a good mother or woman for that matter. Our rageful voices are compressed, silenced, and left to fester beneath the shame, meaning we may find it difficult to unravel our rage. Society tells us that our anger is unhealthy and to be avoided or ignored. When screening for postpartum depression, anger is not in the list of questions to navigate a woman's mental wellbeing.[2]

Symptoms of postnatal rage include:

- Unable to control your temper even for the smallest of things.

- Screaming or swearing more often which is out of character.

- Unable to calm yourself or focus.

- Physically punching or throwing things.

- Violent thoughts which may be directed at your partner or other family members.

- Overthinking or dwelling on something that upsets you.

- Being highly emotional after a physical or rage filled altercation.

This out of character behavior needs professional attention and the sooner support is received the better. As with many elements of emotional and mental distress, postpartum rage is often triggered by something. It may not always be possible to identify the trigger, but by recognizing the rage you will begin to unravel the knots.

Pulling the Threads on Parental Burnout

Parental burnout is on the rise. It is not a particularly great surprise considering we are incessantly overwhelmed, frequently dissatisfied, and worn-out from balancing home life, work-life, and our parental duties. The World Health Organization has classified burnout as an occupational syndrome.[3] While we are paid in cheeky hugs and snotty kisses and find our overtime in sleepless nights, parenting remains one of the most challenging, most under-appreciated jobs ever to exist.

Unlike depression, burnout creeps up gradually as we are routinely triggered, depleted and inundated with demands from every corner. This slow arrival may seem as though we should recognize the gentle slide into burnout but it's the complete opposite. It slowly integrates into our lives and deteriorates our mindset.

Parental burnout is not the makings of the millennial generation raised with soft cushions protecting them from every fall. It is a legitimate concern at a time of our lives that is traditionally exhausting. There is often the expectation that we must simply get on with it, trudge through the rising storm, block those negative feelings that appear, and ignore the building mental and physical fatigue.

If a close friend were suffering from occupational burnout, we would support them, tell them to take time off, encourage self-care, urge them to visit their GP, and ultimately quit that job if it no longer fits. As parents, we are expected to carry on, climb the wall of exhaustion, slip up with frustration, battle with anxiety, and bury the feelings of inadequacy and disconnection. We cannot quit being a mother, not that we would want to, but when distress and fatigue begin to rear their ugly head, we don't have to accept it as being a part of ordinary motherhood and continue to slog through the tough waters of homemade slime and multicolored glittery play dough. Not that I mind making homemade dough, I just can't seem to get the salt to flour ratio right, ending up with either a rough dough or one that won't last a day in the refrigerator.

Parenting is all encompassing as we compete in a world of perfectionism, balancing on the brink of a parental breakdown. Striving for perfection generates a strong risk of developing burnout, as does our stress levels, especially if we are unduly aware of them which is somewhat of a by-product of losing ourselves in motherhood.

Along with developing burnout we can add an unequivocal isolation and loneliness, a vast unrecognizable change in our appearance and our attitudes, and implicit exhaustion, and soon enough we are left balancing so dangerously on the edge. Burnout is not about being dissatisfied with parenthood. It is not about how capable we are of parenting, or a sign of weakness. Instead, it is chronic parental stress as our minds and bodies navigate the consistent overwhelming nature of parenthood.

Burnout has a wonderfully hazardous way of distancing us from our children. Those feelings of being fed up and lost add to a diminishing sense of purpose, which may be something we are already navigating in motherhood. We find that we no longer have a want or need to solve the Rubik's cube, whether we could or not. Even peeling the stickers seems pointless.

It does not, however, mean we have a deteriorating love for our children or that we are worn-out being their parent. It means the constant, always-on nature of parenthood, has become too much which indicates we need help to find a rebalance on life.

Signs we are mentally exhausted or burning out include:

- Being easily irritated and losing our patience quicker than usual.

- Feeling unmotivated or having no interest in things we usually enjoy.

- Having anxiety or panic attacks which may seem to happen for no reason.
- Suffering stomach problems or acid reflux.
- Feeling detached and unable to stay close to people.
- Being exhausted and unable to concentrate.
- Unable to sleep or taking longer to fall asleep.
- Feeling unfulfilled.
- Overwhelmed.

Let's think about if we took the job of motherhood into the office. How would we manage the stress and overwhelm we are experiencing? We would likely talk to a manager, share our burden with colleagues on our lunchbreak, or work with our team to find solutions, ultimately working towards making the role more manageable, if possible.

But we don't have a line manager or an empathetic boss who would graciously encourage us to sign off work for a fortnight. There are no overbearing managers in motherhood, unless you look down past your waist to the tousled hair of your offspring who follow you from room to room to see what you are doing.

And yes, because of burnout, fatigue, and the persistent rollercoaster, we dream about the possibility of quitting this job (even temporarily) with the hope of disappearing to the Bahamas to find ourselves amongst the waves and coconuts. We cannot work our way out of burnout, yet with parenting there is no end to this job. Again, there is no quitting parenting.

There are ways to make life with kids more reasonable, less pressurized, and no, I would never guarantee more energy and sleep, but striking a balance with family life and identifying our triggers and stressors will see a more centered parent. Simple solutions like meal planning, shopping online, avoiding overscheduling, maintaining good and positive habits, and having a backup plan when unexpected events occur like the dreaded vomiting bug. Relieving our stress, overwhelm and by being kind to ourselves is one step towards a new balance.

It is encouraging for us to know that if we become mentally exhausted by parenthood, we do not have to continually force ourselves to carry on, that we are allowed to slow down and recharge our emotionally capacity. We do, after all, routinely give more than we have.

The Vulnerability of Motherhood

This chapter is incredibly complex as we look at mental wellbeing in its entirety. There are excellent books and resources available which encapsulate how to navigate the unrelenting road of postnatal depression, anxiety, obsessive compulsive disorder, post-traumatic stress disorder, postnatal psychosis, and a multitude of mental health challenges. While I gently touch on the overlapping content of depression and my own story, there is no book, no article, no word of advice that can replace that of speaking to your care provider about your mental wellbeing. This conversation must be heavily underlined with the narrative of "It's ok to not be ok" and please seek help. Talk to someone you trust who will guide you to get the help you need in balancing the tumultuous nature of motherhood and the isolating experience of turbulent mental health.

We perhaps do not acknowledge how vulnerable motherhood can make us. Pregnancy and birth physically pick us apart piece by piece and motherhood psychologically reconnects us in a twisted, unrecognizable fashion, rearranging us entirely. There is a beauty and honesty in pregnancy, birth, and motherhood but we are ultimately raw and exposed.

The vulnerability is extreme, and it is only in this exposure, when we are open with each other, that we can connect and empathize with every new bewildered mother who attempts, as we have done, to look much more adept at motherhood than she actually feels. There's a knack to every part of mothering, many of which I either never got the hang of or figured out in my own stumbling way, whether it was toilet training, weaning, or struggling with a good latch and resorting to nipple shields which kept sliding off.

Our mental wellbeing is particularly vulnerable at certain times of our life, of our day even. We sometimes falter and find it a little harder to pull ourselves up because triggers make us anxious, overwhelmed, desperately sad, or panicked. We make mistakes, have worries, and are exhausted, so it's no wonder we feel so vulnerable and respond in ways which hide away our sadness, irritability, or angst.

Unravel

On a scale of 1-10, how mentally exhausted do you feel? 1 being, "What's exhaustion? I'm as fully charged as the baby at 2AM." 10 being, "I'm spent, well and truly spent, like the toddler refusing to walk another inch on the two-minute stroll home from school."

1 2 3 4 5 6 7 8 9 10

I want you to bear in mind as we unravel this chapter that your experience of motherhood is important, necessary, and valid. Your mental wellbeing is also important, necessary, and valid. And no matter what may come up for you in this chapter remember you truly are doing an excellent job. Whatever may trigger a brief lapse of mental agility does not define you or stifle you as a mother or a woman. Understanding our triggers can help us gain greater clarity on who we are as our self-awareness expands, and we look deeper into what makes us tick.

The Triggers of Motherhood

On any given day of motherhood, we experience a range of emotions from excitement at watching our kid cycle unaided for the first time, to frustration when no one eats the dinner we spent two hours cooking. We feel joyful, empowered, sometimes invincible throughout these dynamic shifts of life as a parent. Motherhood is also laden with self-doubt and stress making our emotions complicated and often contradictory but every single one of them is valid as we navigate these days.

When I am talking about triggers, I am referring to those inexplicable moments in our day which lift one finger off the burnout ledge. The moments we were not expecting, the mundane occurrences which outweigh our reactions such as our kids' behavior to an unexpected bill arriving.

I struggled with triggers for years as a new mother. The first time around, when Allegra was just a baby, I was triggered into a belief that I was not a good mother, or that I was a mother who could easily be replaced. I felt embarrassed by how I mothered. I felt incapable. I thought I lacked all mothering knowledge and pearls of wisdom, as though I lost the book every woman was gifted with when her insides shifted to reproduce. I felt patronized as though I was a little girl playing dolls.

These were my feelings. No one handed them to me on a plate with cheese and crackers. No one made me feel this way, but I was triggered into feelings of worthlessness as I failed to recognize I was suffering with postnatal depression.

For those first few years of motherhood, I hovered around being maternal and struggled to commit to this new adventure. Everyone around me seemed to understand my beautiful baby girl while I looked at her questioningly. If she cried and her great aunt picked her up to soothe her, she was better than me. If my friend, who was not a mother at the time, quickly figured out what the rash on Allegra's back was before I had the chance to open Dr. Google, she was better than me. If Barry made her laugh in seconds after I tried all day to get a gurgle out of her, he was better than me. These subtle triggers of inadequacy took a long time to understand and come to terms with.

When Devin came along, the triggers shifted with a mental upheaval and anger and rage poured out of me through the overwhelm, the postnatal depression, and those lingering feelings of failure and incompetence. I screamed, shouted, banged my fists on counters, walls, floors, threw objects, and scared myself.

I have been triggered by moments which seem minimal or inconceivable, pointless to one person but catastrophic to my mental capacity at the time. Loud noises, including the tractors which rumble past our house at midnight when the fields are ready to be harvested, have rattled me to the core. I would become unearthly agitated by any kind of sensory overwhelm which seemed out of place and irritating such as Barry humming or tapping his feet. The feel of silicone cake molds still sends me into a peculiar unrecognized panic as I have struggled to address this trigger and making phone calls or organizing a tradesperson at one stage sent me into a cold sweat. So, I avoided both completely for eighteen months of my postpartum life. Another interesting trigger which countered Barry's experience was seeing a dad out for a walk with his toddler happily cocooned in the Baby Jogger. What my husband saw were his memories of exploring with the kids when they were babies. What I saw, and was justifiably triggered by, was the loneliness and isolation of being a new parent.

Motherhood comes with its own unique set of physical and emotional triggers. The daily mental load and workload can be so oppressive that it causes strong emotional responses. They are varied, often negative responses rooted in an emotional stress, with guilt, anger, sadness, anxiety, or irritability. I saw the danger in myself and worked hard on fighting those triggers and getting well because the intense behavior was entirely reactionary as a result of anxiety. Our triggers are there to protect us. Emotional warning systems set off in our brains creating habits which invariably keep us in a cycle of trigger and reaction and supposed protection. Getting to know our triggers allows us the opportunity to recognize how our mental state is, where we may need support, and what blocks or emotional wounds we need dressing up.

Being triggered by certain aspects of our day does not mean we will explosively react to the situation which has caused an emotional swirl within us, but there is an intense emotional reaction regardless of our mood. It can often be the case that how we respond is bigger than the trivial experience, but the signs may be slight at first until we are triggered repeatedly.

The signs we have been triggered by the kids fighting, the dinner burning, or the cat nimbly curling its way in between our legs can include:

- Feelings of anxiety

- A racing heart

- An upset stomach

- Trembling, shakiness, or dizzy spells

- Hot flushes or cool chills

- An overwhelming need to escape or run away

Motherhood is rewarding and relentless which means we often swing quickly from one emotion to another at a single given time. We are grateful our children are safe and healthy but also irritated by their constant demands. It's the pendulum we feel but may be afraid to voice.

As a mother of two wonderfully mixed-up Rubik's cubes, I have realized that I have attempted to find control in my home, with my kids or Barry, even the routine of my day, so that I am not caught out by the unpredictable nature of parenthood. However, we don't always have to solve every puzzle with which we are faced. The more mixed up my two cubes, the more colorful they are. While I may be routinely triggered by their behavior, that is my problem and not theirs.

We can't rigidly control our environment to avoid these triggers, but we can rewire our brain to react differently when certain things occur. How we think affects how we feel, and how we feel impacts how we interact with the world around us. By challenging and changing our thought patterns we can influence our feelings when triggered and confront unhelpful behavioral patterns which impact on our day.

So, while I have in the past often thought about controlling their behavior, have had perfectionist tendencies, and have struggled with the belief that I am suffering as a result of being a mother, I recognize now that these are my triggers, and I do not need to solve any puzzles but my own. There is no cheating when it comes to being a mother—no guidebooks, action plans, or Human Resources, no matter how often we would like to file a complaint.

This is quite easy to write down as my kids are playing with their dad in the sitting room and much harder, I know, when the baby is crying, the toddler needs their bum wiped, and you realize that you forgot to defrost the dinner. What we are looking at is *responding* rather than *reacting*. To do this we need to unravel our triggers and become more self-aware.

Identifying Our Triggers

We can all be emotionally triggered at some stage or another. We all have a unique rainbow of emotions, reactions, and responses, so how we react is entirely dependent on our personalities, history, relationships, and so much more. It could be something someone said, something they did or didn't do, a place you have been asked to go to, unwanted memories, uncomfortable discussions, or even your own behaviors.

I have become increasingly agitated and anxious in the past when too many demands were put on me. I would retreat and run away because I knew it would trigger a chaotic reaction in me. Being too needed, smothered, feeling judged or criticized, and feeling helpless, have all attributed to the explosive reactions I have had over the years of new motherhood. Learning to counter these reactions and respond appropriately took a long time with deep introspection as to why I reacted in strong ways to such supposed minor events in my life.

When my kids ask for snacks, pencils, drinks, to play with them, more snacks, paint, toys, sweets, and the remaining 215 requests they make of me, I can be incessantly triggered by their constant need of me. I am their mother, of course they need me, but the overwhelm of being irreplaceably needed can trigger a reaction because I was not paying attention to the emotional response I was having. This trigger for a long time was an internal push which I had yet to acknowledge within myself. At the time, I took extraordinarily little care of myself, gave zero time to my own space, and needs, and was overwhelmed by the mental load. It took time for me to learn that this was an opportunity to grow.

Unravel

Are there any triggers from the below list you recognize in your own life?

- Sensory overload—excessive noise, shouting, banging, repetitive barking
- Constant arguing or asking questions
- Not being heard or listened to
- Being lied to
- Being touched out and needing space
- Loneliness or isolation
- A messy house and little support
- Comparing with others and self-doubt
- Exhaustion and fatigue
- Having no time for yourself
- Financial demands
- Relationship demands

What other triggers would you include?

_____

_____

_____

(continued next page)

When identifying areas in your life which you already recognize may trigger or stress you, include as much detail as possible so that if a situation were to trigger you again you will recognize it before you react. Journaling can help to routinely capture these details and give you the opportunity to write down how you are feeling, how you behave, and how you can address the problem in the future.

Learning to understand these responses, the why of the trigger, we can navigate our emotional reaction in a better way. There are a few ways we can do this:

Listen to your body. Certain situations produce strong emotional responses which can rivet through our body as physical sensations. These include a racing heart, feeling dizzy or shaky, sweating, and feeling nauseous. Listen to your body and notice the physical reactions. Have your muscles tensed, is your jaw tight, how deeply are you breathing? When a strong reaction begins, take it as sign to pause before the impulsive reaction takes over.

Listen to your thoughts. Along with these emotional responses your mind may be a jumble of thoughts. What narratives are running through your head? Listen to your thought patterns. Can you separate fact from fiction? What is real and what is reactionary? When strong thoughts begin, take it as another sign to pause before your impulsive thinking pattern takes over.

Notice the reaction. When the reaction occurs, notice the feelings which are conjured up alongside it. What is it about that moment that made you angry or frustrated? Tie the physical and emotional reactions together with your thoughts.

Find the trigger. Connect your reaction to the situation which triggered the reaction. It may have been a loud shriek from one of the kids in the next room, an ill smell from the fridge or your bra strap pulling on your skin. The triggers can be minor in comparison to the reaction or the hidden root cause. We are often unaware what may cause a reaction until we are in the middle of it.

Dig a little deeper. Our triggers may be rooted a little deeper than we imagine. It is worthwhile looking a little further into the experience to see if it connects with any aspect of your life which drifts around an emotional wound. These are issues we have unburdened ourselves of and buried within our psyche. Past events, past relationships, past emotions, and unmet needs can be left to fester and develop into hidden triggers.

Focusing on our triggers, identifying every aspect of them, can help us to navigate those moments in motherhood which appear heartachingly difficult to manage. Allowing our triggers to build and multiply can lead us into a negative spiral of pessimistic thinking and beliefs that we are not good enough, are not worthy, or are broken. We cannot avoid these triggers. As simple and straightforward as that sounds, triggers are there because they are easily accessible. Our minds can easily find more things that can trigger us in a comparable manner as spiraling emotions are a by-product of life.

By working through these triggers, we can unknot them in a way which can help us to heal them, make sense of them, of the situation, of our emotions, and transform our reactions into neutral responses which alleviate any explosive discharge.

Unraveling Our Triggers

We have two options when it comes to managing our triggers. We can avoid the situation and allow the trigger to consume us, our children, and our home life, which, let's face it, will only knot us up tighter in the long run. On the other hand, we can learn a healthier way to unknot those triggers.

Not all triggers are created equal, and some are easier to control than others which again is another reason why navigating your mental wellbeing is best done alongside the support of a professional. Like everything else in this book, this unraveling of our triggers is a process which ultimately may create more knots along the way without adequate support.

So, how can we negotiate with the heightened and perplexing triggers that can take over?

It's OK to feel your emotions. When we are triggered, we feel a surge of emotions that can be overpowering. These feelings are all valid and it is ok to feel what's happening for you in the moment. We cannot deny or ignore our emotions. Instead, we can rationalize them and try to understand why they are cropping up in such a way. Ask yourself if there is something which occurred in your past that is related to the present moment? For example, if you yelled at your son, have you been triggered as you remember being shouted at in the same manner as a child?

Avoid jumping to conclusions. Most of the time our interactions with others are not meant to be harmful or upsetting. If a friend commented on the way you hold your baby, their intentions may not be sinister but objective, even caring. However, you may be triggered in a way that makes you feel inadequate. It is easy to misinterpret people's actions, so keep an open mind in how you navigate events, conversations, and your own thought patterns.

Take a time out. Triggers are both physically and emotionally overwhelming. If it suits you to take yourself out of the scenario to calm your body and mind, it is perfectly ok to do this. Breathing and grounding exercises can help to regain your cool and make sense of the situation and how it triggered you. Reflect on what you need in the moment.

Work on your self-awareness. Self-awareness is a skill that does not develop overnight. Strengthening our individual understanding of ourselves helps us to understand what parts of our life we need to work on and identify our strengths. In doing this, we can help manage our triggers by understanding our weaknesses, redefining our boundaries, and taking a step back to see the bigger picture of our life. We can fill in the blanks by supporting ourselves and giving to ourselves what we need in that moment.

Unravel

Here are some questions to ask yourself when you feel yourself becoming triggered to help you be more self-aware:

- What is going on in my body? For example, clenched jaw, sweating, trembling.
- What emotions am I feeling? For example, hurt, rejected, sad, angry.
- What happened?
- Am I understanding the situation correctly?
- Has a boundary been crossed?
- What do I need to overcome this trigger?
- What do I need in this moment?

The Parental Pause

I asked chartered psychologist Allison Keating, a prominent and well-respected practitioner in Ireland to help unknot our mental wellbeing and to give clarity on how we can manage the overwhelming triggers of motherhood. Allison has spent more than twenty years destigmatizing mental health issues and is a major advocate of positive psychology. I have long trusted her opinion and expertise and her book *The Secret Lives of Adults* was an eye-opening read for me throughout my experience of ailing mental health. Her words helped realign my attitude to my relationship with myself as I learnt to nurture the one person I was neglecting.

"Read that line again," she says to me as we talk about the triggers of motherhood, and we work through this chapter and unravel our mental wellbeing. "I am not alone in being triggered by intense parenting moments," I say, reading aloud the opening line of *Unraveling Triggers*, and she beams a knowing smile. Allison asks me to pause, longer still, to hold that moment a little deeper, and to breathe. We sit with this idea for a time until she says, "When triggered, what you need in your psychological toolbox is the 'parental pause' and to actively remember this as it will be hard. What most feel in triggered moments is alone and ashamed. It's time to break that myth."

Managing the parental pause is not quite so simple as stopping, standing still, breathing, and allowing the moment to wash over you. "How do you feel when you are triggered?" Allison asks and she sums it up in a few short words, "angry and frustrated and hot and upset and full of emotion with a swirling sense of feeling out of control and dysregulated." Dysregulated may be my new favorite word as it conjures up the entire whirlwind of being triggered.

"The intensity is the cue," she says and guides me through a practice to calm the heightened and overpouring emotions. "You need to ask with compassion and curiosity, why am I so upset, angry, or frustrated right now?" In knowing the emotion and its strength, we can then alleviate the triggered response in a few steps which Allison walks us through: **Step 1:** If it is safe to do so (if your children are ok to be left safely for a few minutes or in a cot), go somewhere you can self-soothe. If at home the bathroom will do just fine.

Step 2: Take a deep breath in and release. Breathe in for four, hold for four and release for four this sends a signal to your brain that you are safe and it's ok to for your body and nervous system to calm down.

Step 3: Tune into your body. What is present right now? Is your heart beating fast, are you breathing faster, are there a lot of thoughts running through your mind, can you feel the adrenaline coursing through your body?

Step 4: Accept how you feel and ask yourself softly like a kind parent would to a child, "what is upsetting you?"

Step 5: Allow any emotions to come up, feelings of shame, fear, guilt, feelings of not being good enough or like a bad mother. Notice if you can feel this in your body. It can feel stuck and nearly hurt in your throat. Place your hands gently on your throat, or your chest if you feel it there. Close your eyes and allow any emotions to move up and allow a release through tears or a big sigh or both.

Step 6: If you have time, revisit it twenty minutes later to give your nervous system a chance to regulate. Get out a notebook and write out what triggered you and why. Leave judgement aside. Imagine yourself as an external observer and note what you saw. Breathe space into the emotions that come up for you. This is a free association technique. It will not be poetic or beautifully written prose. It will be illegible and written with ferocity, frustration, and lots of curse words. Write and write until you feel nearly a physical release that may be accompanied by an audible sigh or "oh, that's what has upset me."

And herein lies an old wound that sits in front of us in black and white on creased and marked paper. Allison advises at this stage to do some compassionate triage by assessing the emotional wound.

She says to ask ourselves:

- What is this emotional wound?
- Where did it begin?

- What is it bringing up for me?

- What is it about the situation that triggered me?

- What emotion or narrative has been activated?

- Listen to your inner voice.

- How can I heal this wound?

"Often, accepting the situation as it is as opposed to how you would have liked it to be is the key," Allison says. "Gently identifying the unmet need and re-parenting will soothe the wound. You know you've been triggered. You've triaged and assessed the emotional wound. Next step is re-parenting. Re-parenting yourself allows you to heal any unmet childhood needs. Inner-child work is deeply cathartic and transformative. There are so many reasons why parents don't meet their children's emotional needs. It is always helpful to be mindful of the historical context and norms when thinking of your own parents. There can be inter-generational trauma that unfortunately gets passed down unless therapeutic or personal trauma informed work is done."

Unravel

"Re-parenting is some of the most important healing work you can do," says Allison, "and will benefit you and everyone in your family. Even though it will be hard, it is the most worthwhile work."

If you can, imagine a Russian doll, your inner child at the core with you wrapped around her with your past, present and unconscious self. Imagine the influence of your parents, siblings, and society as you begin to find your true self and unravel and unknot what doesn't serve you anymore and give yourself the freedom to parent and live your own authentic life.

If you have identified the emotion or narrative of 'I am not good enough' or 'I am a failure' go back to the point when this was activated for you. Close your eyes and remember what happened if it isn't too traumatic. If it is, do this with support in therapy. Connect to what the emotion was and then ask, "What did I need in that moment in time?"

_____

_____

_____

Imagine yourself as you are now, coming towards your younger self, see what age you were and visualize bending down and gently reassuring yourself with a gentle hug. As the adult, you acknowledge the hurt and pain that occurred and then let your inner child know they will be ok, that they are very loved and that you are more than enough. This work will need to be done on a continuum as your children will hit off old emotional wounds, this is your work and separating what they have done or the noise to what is happening to you is the work of soothing and healing your nervous system.

The Mindset of Motherhood

No matter where we are in our motherhood, we are continually growing. It may not feel like it as we're stuck in a constant momentum between the dried Weetabix on our sleeve and the mismatched Lego figures rinsing in the dishwasher. We try to be present, in the moment, and productive in order to get the most out of these days and prove something to either ourselves or others that we can do this job. But of course, we can. We do not need to prove it. We are doing it. We are possibly doing it under a dark cloud of porous mental health concerns, but no matter the challenges we face throughout motherhood, we are finding our way through every day.

There is no doubt that motherhood is complex and alters our mental energies, but we are not stagnant beings rocking from one day to the next, stuck at the top of the rollercoaster. We can either allow the rollercoaster to carry on its fixed route, or be open to the direction changing, the speed altering, the highs being higher and the lows lower, and grow with the journey. We are controlling the damn thing. We make it go up and the momentum of life can make it go down, the kids create the loops, our partner may hold the rail with us, and we all scream and laugh, close our eyes, or open them wildly.

Motherhood began with growth at a very natural level as our baby formed. Since then, every day has contained and created a fluctuating change whether it is our kids growing up overnight or our recognition of a change of pattern in ourselves. There are constant adjustments and how we interact to those variations will determine how we view our motherhood and the unexpectant events which can trigger us.

We can have what psychologist Carol Dweck calls a "fixed mindset" where we remain unchanged when challenges confront us. Or we can take those challenges and use them to grow, change, and empower ourselves. This is called a "growth mindset" and Dweck sees it as making the conscious decision to learn when we are tackled by obstacles, criticism, and setbacks. When our five-year-old retaliates and refuses to do as we ask, do we struggle to defuse the situation and blame ourselves for our child's behavior or do we say, "Ok, that absolutely sucked," as they storm off to their room, "how can I manage this better next time?" We recognize that the challenges may be hard but there is opportunity within them to navigate life with kids because they are constantly changing. If we stop growing, we will never catch up to their continued growth. Believing our capabilities, skills, and intelligence are not fixed but adaptable, can be developed, expanded, and explored is a distinct message in unraveling how we view our world around us. It gives us a pertinent life skill to take the challenges and run with them.

Adopting a growth mindset begins with having the motivation and desire to step into the uncomfortable, the vulnerable, and to embrace it. This enthusiasm to change and grow is what will help us navigate the intensity of being a parent, of questioning ourselves, of banishing guilt, and allowing ourselves to be human, to make mistakes, and learn from them. Motivation, however, can be limited and so we need to work on our discipline and willpower, eventually evolving into a habit.

Remember:

- Giving yourself time and care is never a selfish act
- Don't cover up your sadness
- Stay in the moment
- Let it out
- Stop thinking about the future
- Embrace vulnerability
- Find the beauty in the moments

Throughout this entire conversation I want you to remember that we do not need to grow, learn, or be challenged in isolation. We do not need to make things more difficult for ourselves. Our growth can mean asking for help from friends and family. It can mean finding childcare or hiring a cleaner. It can mean paying the neighbor's kids to mow the lawn over the summer months which I unashamedly do. It can most certainly mean lowering our standards, alleviating our expectations, and being strategic about finding time for ourselves.

chapter 4

Unraveling Flaws

● **Flaws** \ 'flȯ \
an imperfection or weakness and especially one that
detracts from the whole or hinders effectiveness
Dictionary, **Merriam-Webster**

I AM A FLAWED HUMAN being. I am a flawed mother. And that's ok. Saying this out loud could quite possibly be the best gift I can give you on these pages because we don't always hear this kind of vulnerable truth. When we admit to something so utterly human, it almost feels like permission to let go of trying to be more than we are and accept the entirely passionate, dedicated, and imperfectly wonderful person we are. To say, "I am flawed and that's ok," is a vulnerability like no other because we ask ourselves to recognize our own misgivings and most importantly how they may affect those around us. Being flawed and acknowledging those flaws means we are open to learning and those flaws challenge us to look inward, to unravel.

Now, the dictionary definition may sound utterly critical and the idea that our effectiveness as we parent is in any way hindered can send an already anxious mother into complete hopelessness. I know because

I have been there. I have looked in the mirror and witnessed a woman struggling to mother, to connect, to move on. I saw a one-sided story because flaws and weaknesses have a way of jumping center stage, illuminated in all their inflated minutiae. So, I am not here to tell you that you are flawed but rather that you are an almighty woman overcoming some of the inanest challenges. We can forget that parenting is explicitly complex, that we cannot fix everything, and that we do not know or understand everything.

I have anxiety. I bite my nails. I get angry when I can't focus my thoughts. I avoid imaginative play with the kids 99% of the time. I shut down when I'm losing an argument. I get distracted easily. I'm stubborn. I often give up trying to feed my kids carrots and peas because sausages and mash potato is easier. I sweat profusely when nervous and being uneasy is second nature to me. I struggle with delegating yet whine when not supported. I consistently make lists, meaning I procrastinate. I lie to the kids (mostly about playgrounds being closed in winter) and use the kids as an excuse for my introverted self to decline invitations. I break promises because brain fog seizes up my memory and I am perpetually fatigued.

As I say, I am flawed and incredibly human. Our flaws make us real, give us humanity, and add to the plot twists of our life. How boring would it be if we are all so perfectly ideal?

Parenthood does not create new shortcomings in our lives. They have always been there. However, they may not have manifested themselves in the obvious ways as they do now. They were subtle flaws in our pre-child days, not overly apparent, although certainly there in bucket loads and quite often accepted as being simply benign character traits. For me, there was (and still is) a mixture of insecurity, nervousness, potential gullibility, and the added traits of being timid yet rageful, naïve, and a perfectionist. And while I'm being honest, I was and am unyielding, dubious, contradictory, and sometimes withdrawn. The point is, whatever flaws I had back then affected only me, and I was too unconcerned to notice them.

Parenthood has a funny little way of making these flaws more evident. Most likely because they do not align with our self-imposed ideal, or the clichés we aim to live up to.

It wasn't until the responsibility of caring for another human was added to my CV (because it's one hell of a job worthy of a significant note on our resumé) that my flaws and insecurities came gushing out. My weaknesses were suddenly obvious and likely exaggerated, however they most certainly had an intolerable effect on me and those I was accountable for. Anxiety, and the multitude of complex fragmented associated behaviors, for a significant period of my life stopped me from going anywhere on my own with two kids. Walks in the park, playgrounds, collecting shells on the beach, anywhere further than our back garden was put on hold unless I had the comforting support of Barry or my mum. It meant my conditioning put a pause on my kids' experiences. Any struggle I had caused frustration to spill over and, more times than I'd care to admit, my kids got the brunt of those emotional outbursts. Certain aspects of my flaws affected their little lives, which I may not be happy to admit, but I cannot hide this fact as I unravel my own flaws.

And so, these shortcomings got into my head because the idea of being flawed while also being a mother didn't seem to connect very well to me. Mothers are perfect. Mothers know all. Mothers don't need to lean on the wall to catch their breath. My imperfections solidified in this internal monologue which suggested I become a better, less flawed version of myself because that was what my kids needed. That's what a mother was. Not someone who lost her temper, got frustrated, had an outpouring of emotions, or was a "bad mom" on occasion. But that was me, and many of those flaws are part of my personality and unchangeable. They make me who I am. Other areas can most certainly be worked on, but as those flaws come to light, we can learn to navigate the intricacies of our personality.

Being flawed makes us human. We have our own traumas, insecurities, and obstacles in life, and we do the best we can, with the tools we have, to work through those instances. Agonizing over our emotional blind spots and limitations of character is not going to help us parent any better but unraveling our flaws will. The thing is, we are all likely to make mistakes when it comes to our kids and life in general, but we will also do our damn hardest to get it right. It is along that fine line in between making mistakes and trying our best that we must look. That's where the "perfectly imperfect parent" dances a merry tune.

Unravel

What do you see when you look in the mirror? Do you catch the shadow of what you consider to be inadequacy? Do you pinpoint flaws before you find the kindness in your face? Do you even catch your own reflection at all?

Learning to look at ourselves in the mirror and truly see ourselves increases our self-compassion, improves our relationship with ourselves and others, builds our emotional resilience so we are not knocked down so easily, and helps to manage the lingering stress or strain of motherhood. Getting to know and understand ourselves instils a stronger sense of self as we learn to acknowledge and accept our emotions, thoughts, and be honest with ourselves.

With meditation we usually find ourselves closing our eyes and reflecting inward. With mirror meditation, we hold our gaze. Coming face to face with ourselves is powerful, even for five minutes at a time. This daily practice can completely change how you see yourself.

1. Find a quiet place with a large enough mirror so you do not have to hold it.

2. Sit comfortably in a chair or on the floor.

3. Close your eyes and take several deep breaths.

4. Release any tension in your body with every breath.

5. As you relax, return to breathing naturally.

6. Open your eyes and look into the mirror. Pay attention to your breathing. Has it changed as you gaze into the mirror?

7. What do your eyes tell you? Are you sad, awkward, uncomfortable? Do you find difficult to hold your gaze?

8. What thoughts come to mind? Are you pointing out your imperfections? Do you find yourself being critical of yourself?

9. As each thought and feeling comes up, notice it, and let it pass.

10. Allow your thoughts travel to where they need to go. Continue to hold your gaze. Look at yourself with kindness.

Imperfection

When it comes to parenting, we need only get it right half the time according to research by Dr. Susan Woodhouse, published in the journal *Child Development*.[1] I can undoubtedly get on board with that considering I am pulled from hour to hour, room to room, and fridge to whatever press the biscuits are in, by my two ever-demanding kids with guilt being a ubiquitous force stagnating the room. Throughout all the pulling, pushing, and shoving, I don't always make the right choices, especially when my mental capacity is particularly diminished by the all-consuming daily demands, and the constant touching. It took me a long time to come to terms with the fact that kids are very tactile.

Left feeling constantly challenged by motherhood and the idea that we have to know what we are doing when we do it, and smash the bullseye while we're at it, I wondered why I needed to be on target, ideal, or minutely perfect all the time. There are days when I feel warped and cracked about how I am mothering, leading to feeling so painfully inadequate that I cannot keep up with what is expected of me. And I certainly can't give up. There's no giving up as a parent. It's not like we can hand back the keys to the manual Ford Focus and ask for a trade in, preferably automatic.

Instead, I try to up my game, but here's where I get stuck. I have levelled up as best I can. I have nothing left to give and only mistakes left to make through my overwhelmed and exhausted body. So where is this magic line between doing my best and doing what is needed of me because on my flow chart the lines do not quite match up.

This is the thing; parenting is insanely hard. It's also insanely flawed. How can we get it right all the time when we are faced with independent, unique personalities who are as controllable as a tub of soup in the microwave? However, if parenting was idealistically straightforward without the immense challenges it throws at us, it may not be as rewarding as it can be.

My idea of what parenthood entails changed rapidly from those original ill-conceived and ill-prepared thoughts I first had. I had anticipated being an easy-going mum who recycled the ice pop sticks to make finger puppets to entertain a pre-walker with creative stories about mermaids, castles, and dragons because the three apparently go well together. I expected to know what every sad cry meant, how to miraculously heal grazed knees and make the most delicious and healthy purees even an adult would crave. I swore I would not get frustrated, angry, or anxious over every obstinate parenting trial like a two year old who refuses to sleep between the hours of 2 and 5 am, or a toddler who would only eat pale foods or red cheese. I would know precisely what my children needed and never get it wrong, because getting it wrong meant I was failing, and I wasn't going to fail. To me this was a good mother, and it seemed my vision board was attainable. It wasn't.

Being a flawed mother, failing on occasion was inevitable but it's not the dictionary definition of flaws or failure either. There is nothing implicit about getting things wrong as a parent. It is not failure. It is adapting, learning, and growing inward or outward or whatever way you need to grow as a human raising tiny humans.

So, I am not that easy going mum, but rather one who sits on high alert in a suspended state of manageable anxiety. While I love arts and crafts with the kids, my efforts are not Insta worthy and usually end up lamenting in landfill a week later. I superglued my fingers together, along with neon yellow feathers, when I had notions about those finger puppets. I hushed and shushed a crying baby not knowing if she was teething, hungry, annoyed by my face gawping at her yet again, or simply as exhausted as I was. I mashed avocado twice, freezing little blocks in the ice cube tray, and wasn't too surprised when I found them ten months later still frozen and completely inedible.

Years into this parenting dynamic, I have gotten it wrong more times than I can count, often before breakfast or at least by the time I'm scraping the dried Shreddies into the bin again. Small moments of apparent failure pick away at me until something else I "failed" to do comes along to replace it. Weekly errors and epic moments that haunt you as you promise to learn from them.

It turns out, getting it wrong is perfectly okay and most certainly not a failure, but I will admit that I have given myself a hard time over 95% of these mistakes, especially the big ones, such as the day I could not tell if eighteen-month-old Devin had swallowed limescale remover after finding her happily toddling around the house with the container in her mouth, sucking on it like her 1pm milk bottle. A six-hour sojourn in A&E confirmed she hadn't. I tortured myself over leaving the dangerous detergent on the bathroom floor within easy reach of her inquisitive toddler hands. But I failed to praise myself for my quick thinking in contacting the poisons helpline, picking her sister up from school, and heading directly to the hospital, all while anxiety ripped my insides as I kept a calm, smiling front for the kids.

Then there was the day her little two-year-old finger was caught in the car door after a split-second decision mistook how far away she was from the car. Devin lost a nail and not a finger, but I took the entire blame for the incident and took a long time to forgive myself for being human.

Amidst my efforts to be the best I could be, I found I was burning out from trying so hard. My mental lethargy was not from the continuous demands, crying marathons, or the mountainous to-do list. My physical and mental exhaustion was exacerbated by not knowing how to unravel my own intricacies, flaws, and humanity against this idea of perfection or the need to get it right. I was fighting against my human inadequacies and not accepting myself for who I am.

I pushed to be a perfect parent but was blisteringly unaware of the idea of being a "good enough" mother. Motherhood is not about perfection, but rather accepting what you are capable of.

Good Enough

We cannot and should not expect or be expected to be "always on," constantly managing and monitoring the needs of everyone else as our own needs slip down around our ankles like the poorly elasticated socks we bought seven years ago (because the sock and underwear drawers of a mother are usually older than her children). I have been caught out enough times thinking I was failing as one kid cried the house down and the other carved a stick figure into the dining table with a surprisingly sharp, bright pink, plastic Play-Doh tool. In some ways, that rough attempt at making her mark on our furniture is a steady reminder that it's ok if I drop the ball every now and again.

Let's think back a moment to our grandmother's era of juggling children and happy homes, the British pediatrician and psychoanalyst Donald Winnicott, coined the phrase "good enough" parenting, defending the ordinary mother (in those days, the mother was often the primary carer, and so the reference is to the maternal figure) from outside influences that allegedly aim to help us in this rollercoaster of parenthood.[2] Winnicott essentially gave us permission to not be perfect and eased the minds of mothers who attempted to be more and do more than they physically and mentally could.

In comparison to mothering in the 1950s, the external influences of negative comparisons are piling higher and higher on our modern-day shoulders. We are met with an onslaught of advice and the "right way" to raise our kids. With friends, family, influencers, and social media judging us and throwing their opinions at us, we are inundated with a belief that we can (or even should) be bigger and better, to give our all and leave nothing for ourselves, to aim high because we can "have it all." These voices silence our own so we can no longer hear our own beliefs or see our path in motherhood.

The good-enough paradigm is a much-needed release from being perfect and from chastising ourselves for being in any way flawed. It is a school of thought that I have clung to quite tightly in recent years as I unraveled motherhood and gave myself permission to recognize that I cannot match up to certain ideals.

We know our parenting efforts influence how our babies develop. Unsurprisingly, we think anything less than perfect will have an undesirable effect. However, the idea of attachment theory is that we give our babies and young children the confidence that we are readily available to comfort, protect, and support them. Blending that idea in with "good enough" allows us to recognize that we are allowed to possibly get it wrong. We are human after all. Mistakes do not negate our attachment but rather reinforce the independence of our children, helping them to develop a sense of "me."

Woodhouse, an associate professor at Lehigh University, focuses on the applications of attachment theory to children's and adolescents' relationships with parents. She suggests in her research that the development of the secure attachment between mother and newborn need not be as immediate or as faultless as we generally believe. As new parents, we think we need to pick up the crying baby, figure out their needs, and answer their call. If we don't get it right fifty percent of the time, that's ok. Woodhouse supposes that to develop that secure attachment, like Winnicott's belief, we do not need to be the constantly "on" mother.

To be a regular and devoted parent, we can find a balance between the pressures of parenthood, the guilt we are consumed by, and the fact that we are not superhuman. We can get it wrong. Reminding ourselves that we are permitted to fail, to try again, and be imperfect, is the key to balancing our own growth as a parent as well as our child's psychological development in learning to deal with frustration, disappointment, and the reality of life outside of the bubble of the attached parent.

The Problem with the Perfect Parent

The tricky thing about attempting to be a perfect parent is that when we make mistakes, those mistakes seem bigger. A small blunder is deemed much greater than it is, and we guilt ourselves with our supposed parenting fail, as though we are coming up short and try to catch up, even though making mistakes is all part of our learning—for us and for our children.

"Good enough" gets a bit of criticism because it is misinterpreted. Some believe it is about dropping our standards, letting go, or giving up on certain aspects of parenting, which I think we can agree is not the case. "Good enough" is about realizing our capabilities, preventing burn out, and avoiding being overwhelmed. It is about knowing that there is only so much we can do as a parent. It is not berating ourselves for needing time alone to switch off and not feeling guilty when things don't go as planned or we don't know the answer.

A good enough parent is about showing warmth and sensitivity to our children, responding to their needs physically and emotionally. It is also about knowing that we cannot routinely sustain a strong perpetual motion of parenthood at a perfect level. It is about being confident in the choices we make as parents and trusting our gut.

Being good enough is about mostly getting it right, and sometimes getting it wrong. And knowing that fingernails grow back!

Perfectly Imperfect

Dr. Mary O'Kane is a wonderful advocate for the "Good Enough" parent. For years I have embraced her words of wisdom like a perfectly knitted shawl wrapped around my shoulders. During the peak of my experience with anxiety I attended a talk where she stood center stage and, in all her brilliant glow of maternal understanding, she talked to the audience about childhood anxiety. At the time, I was already a mother of two starting out on an ambitious career path as I worked from home, an adult by all intents and purposes, but every word she said spoke to me. Her knowledge and awareness of how our minds work helped me to rationalize the intensity of my experience, understand my role as a mum, and find the compassion for myself which I duly lost. This was all in between how she spoke about our children's lives that are increasingly consumed by stress and anxiety and how to support them.

Mentally, I was on the verge of unraveling, but I wasn't quite there yet. I credit Mary with pulling that first thread for me as she unknowingly started to unravel what I felt was a bitter, all-consuming, internal flaw—anxiety. I took my fear, nervousness, worry, and anxiousness personally. For me it was a pattern of improper behavior that I made, controlled, and continued, ignoring the fact that my mental wellbeing was standing on a cliff edge. The internal and external voices of reason and control fought very heavily in my mind, and yet I took the blame for this overbearing human flaw. It was a time in my life when I felt broken and unfixable, when neither of those words should have been in my vocabulary. That is until Mary, standing five rows in front of me, explained in detail the science behind what was going on in my mind and gently pulled that thread.

Little did I know as I sat in that audience that Mary would become a firm friend. Someone I wholeheartedly trust and am inspired by. I was honored to be her editor as she wrote her first book, *Perfectly Imperfect*

Parenting: connection not perfection, and I found myself entangled in her words of how to connect with our children and join the dots with our idea of motherhood. This connection is an element of this unraveling as we figure out how we want to parent in a way that matches our personality and beliefs.

Mary's vision of parenting counters those ideologies which are heavily placed in our society. As a mother of three, she has the experience, and as a parenting and childhood educator she has the backing and understanding of research. Talking to Mary about my perception of motherhood as we walk the Hill of Tara in County Meath, a vast and sprawling landscape once the seat of the High Kings of Ireland, her words travelling on the wind unknotted me. It is in the raw and honest, often impromptu conversations about motherhood that show us that while we may stay knotted in some areas, we are unraveling in others, and yet simultaneously stitching up as we learn and grow comfortable in our motherhood. We are not looking to eradicate ourselves of flaws but to recognize that they are there and accept these misplaced misgivings, to recognize who we are, and be comfortable in being "perfectly imperfect."

"I have a strong belief that parents today, most specifically mothers, are put under immense pressure from society to be perfect," Mary tells me as we talk about this idea of unraveling not for the first time. "It seems impossible to avoid that pressure, so it is no wonder we feel so imperfect. The standards set for mothers are so high that we spend most of our parenting lives trying to reach for the unattainable, thereby setting ourselves up for failure. We know that the generations of parents who came before us were not put under the same pressure to be perfect as we are today. Indeed, the idea of parenting being used as a goal-directed verb is a relatively new concept. We now view parenting as a kind of work which we hope will produce the perfect child. We forget that there is no such thing as perfection when it comes to family life. Perfection is an illusion."

Mary's insight into the idea of being perfectly imperfect is explicit and comforting. She helps unravel and balance the ideas of seeking approval from others, overscheduling our lives, and embracing our vulnerability and imperfection in motherhood.

Seeking Approval

"The big difficulty with seeking perfection is that it is so closely linked to seeking approval," Mary says." We worry about the judgement of other parents and this impacts on our mothering, and therefore our children. Our perfectionism is leading to changes in parenting which impact our children negatively, resulting in children with a fear of failure, a fear of mistakes, and a fear of not meeting the expectations of society."

We know from research that mental health difficulties are rising in children with concerns that these levels are linked to the way we parent in a world full of expectation, deliberate rules, and a gender inequality. Jean Twenge, Professor of Psychology at San Diego State University, examined five decades of surveys on teen attitudes and behaviors in the United States in 2017.[3] The findings of this study are as interesting today as they were then as the same behaviors are expounded year on year.

"Twenge found that iGen (teenagers born after 1995) were reporting unprecedented levels of anxiety, depression and loneliness as compared to previous generations," Mary says. "Interested in why these levels were rising at such an alarming rate, she delved further into other changes over this period to consider their impact. Two specific findings really stand out for me. In psychology, we speak about 'locus of control'—a person's sense of control over their world. Five decades ago, teens were likely to have an internal locus of control, which means they felt that their lives were controlled by their own efforts. Twenge found that modern day teens no longer felt a personal sense of control over their world, particularly worrying when we know that this control is linked to mental health issues. She also found that in the same period there was a change from a focus on intrinsic goals (involving personal development and relationships) to more extrinsic goals (linked to material gain, status, and validation from others). It seems our teens today feel that they have little control over their lives and are also very reliant on external sources of validation."

But how does this relate to our quest for perfection? As with Twenge's research, our focus is on the changes in generational thinking.

Over-Scheduling, Over-Protecting

As parents, our primary concern is to protect our children and maintain their physical and mental wellbeing but how we parent today is impacting on our children's development.

"Professor Peter Grey of Boston University argues that we over-schedule and over-protect our children," says Mary, "most importantly, depriving them of opportunities for free play.[4] Free play has long been proven to be essential to our children's social and emotional development, it provides opportunities to develop important skills that cannot be learned in adult directed activities. It is the means through which children learn problem-solving and conflict resolution skills, how to bargain and negotiate, social skills and lessons about friendship. Previous generations allowed their children the freedom to engage in activities which developed these skills. They saw themselves as parents, but they did not see their role as being ever-present."

In our mother and grandmother's generations, children were allowed freedoms that our children today may never experience. But once this pressure for perfection overwhelmed us, we became the playdate generation.

"We were sold the story that if we were the perfect parent," says Mary, "ever present, protecting our children, they would come to no harm.

And so, we became controlling. Controlling every variable meant we could outrun risk. We were seeking a black and white world, a world of certainty, where our children could come to no harm. But this attitude to risk did our children no favors. We have created the perfect storm. We drive our children everywhere, we overschedule their lives, we warn them about all the perceived dangers in the world. By the time they are teenagers they have grown up with a very consistent message that the world is a dangerous place. Then we wonder why levels of anxiety and depression are rising so quickly!"

This idea of seeking approval, over-protecting, and over-scheduling our children and our lives is heavily related to our quest for protection and very much comes down to how we value ourselves within the family unit.

"For so many mothers today," says Mary, "our self-worth is very closely linked to perfection in our parenting role. We are the parents who really struggle with vulnerability, we are the parents who worry about what others will say if we are seen to be imperfect. We are the parents with the inner voice reminding us that we are not good enough. We need to learn to answer back those inner negative voices. Good enough is good enough. There is a wealth of research to support the assertion that being that one good adult in a child's life supports resilience. Note, not the one *perfect* adult, the one *good* adult!"

Embracing Imperfection

And so, Mary's advice is simple yet overtly complex and complicated— Embrace imperfection and let go. While this is something we know will help us, it is entirely a different story when we are asked to look inward and unravel our idea about what we are capable of and how we would wish to be viewed by the outside world.

"Embracing the idea of imperfection goes against everything we have been taught about motherhood" says Mary. "Letting go of the need for perfection doesn't come easily to most of us. It takes time. We need to remind ourselves after one of those very imperfect days that we have faced challenges and survived them. We have made mistakes and learned from them. We have stumbled and picked ourselves up again. We have coped with the trials and tribulations of everyday life, and persevered. We have modelled the behavior we want our children to learn thereby fostering resilience and cultivating perseverance. We have shown them that we are flawed, we are human, we make mistakes, and all of this is part of the human condition. We are imperfect, and they have the right to be imperfect too."

Unravel

The argument that Dr Mary O'Kane is putting towards us is that parenting is not about perfection. Instead, it is about being there for your child. Letting go of the ideal is not easy but possible. She says:

If we want to let go of our inner need for perfection, most of us need to look externally too. For me, social media was a starting point. If we are scrolling endlessly through other mothers' seemingly perfect lives, it usually causes us to feel inadequate. Avoiding, or at the very least limiting time spent looking at social media helps.

We also need to remember that for a mother who is unraveling, asking for help can be so difficult. Let's try to 'reach in' to mothers we feel might be struggling instead of always expecting those struggling to reach out. Let's try to support each other without judgement.

(continued next page)

Letting go of the constraints of perfection, allowing ourselves to be good enough mothers, mothers who try their best, but are flawed, imperfect human beings, could help us to parent in a more present way. It could help us to focus on keeping our children as safe as necessary, rather than as safe as possible. Taking a safe as necessary approach can help support our children to grow in confidence, resilience, and reach their full potential. We can relinquish some of the control in the relationship, step back a little, and instead of controlling, we can scaffold their development.

Let's see ourselves as clues to the crossword—we don't need to give our children the answers to life's challenges, instead we give them a little support to negotiate their way through them. We can be there to support when needed but also encourage independence and bravery.

Finally, instead of seeking perfection, we can seek connection with our children. Instead of seeing parenting as an expertise to be acquired, we can view it as linked to maintaining our relationship with our children, maintaining connection and the invisible string that binds us together.

Finding Those Not So Fatal Flaws

Characters in stories have minor and fatal flaws. Without flaws, characters are boring, the story remains stagnant, and every page reads the same. Give a character some oddities and intricacies and they come alive, lighting up the pages with how they walk, flick a switch, or say the word "situation." Give them a flaw so imposing that it forces the story along. Flaws, imperfections, and character failings set our characters apart while a fatal flaw stops our character from succeeding.

I don't believe, as mothers, we have a large and looming fatal flaw that stops us from being the mother, woman, or person we want to be. We may, on the other hand, have a multitude of not so fatal flaws.

Little things like biting our nails, putting the empty milk carton back in the fridge, and grinding our teeth are funny little quirks; while being late, daydreaming, and procrastinating are not particularly helpful. I love a good daydream though and so I wholeheartedly accept that I can get lost in my own little world. I don't think this is a terribly audacious flaw that I need to fix. Not all flaws need fixing. I am evidently very good at procrastinating considering this book was written as close to deadline day as possible, but then under pressure is when creative juices tend to flow. Again, not the worst flaw. While I am not the person who puts the sweet wrappers back in the box, or the empty carton in the fridge, I don't hold it against my eldest child who does! Our flaws are our intricacies, our plot lines, and they make us who we are.

Overthinking or thinking negatively about ourselves, not believing in ourselves, or not admitting to our flaws can have an altering impact on us that might add several knots to our thread. The more we ignore or agonize over certain personality traits, the tighter the knot gets, and soon enough there is no way around the knot. Unraveling our flaws means accepting things about ourselves we cannot change, recognizing that being flawed makes us human, and knowing that being perfect is not possible.

Unravel

If you are so inclined, take a moment to consider what your flaws may possibly be. However, remember it is much easier to find fault with someone other than ourselves, so it is not as simple as asking, "what are my faults, flaws, or weaknesses?" We have a natural instinct to stroke our ego, protect ourselves, and subjectively deny the truth.

Make a list of your mistakes at the end of the day. Or perhaps just three mistakes to get you started in recognizing that perfection is not implied in motherhood.

_____

_____

_____

View yourself as others do. Take a moment to pause and notice your actions and understand how a friend or neighbor may see you.
Be mindful of your actions, routines, and thoughts. Much of what we do is on autopilot meaning there are large chunks of our day when we are unaware of our actions. Becoming more mindful of ourselves helps us to recognize when and where we may make mistakes, highlighting that no one is perfect.

The Problem with Holding on to Our Flaws

One of the thickest threads I have pulled on motherhood is the idea that I have to try to fix myself. However, I am not broken. I am not failing. Yet somehow the idea that I wasn't "good enough" in my early motherhood, or that I wasn't trying hard enough, ate away at me. Internally, I tried to fix how I parented and fix my personality in line with that. I followed instructions from others whose lives and ideals were so far removed from my own. In fact, some were strangers, or friends with no children who believed they knew it all because of younger siblings or nieces and nephews. Everyone has an opinion and I listened to them all, except my own. I even smiled politely at a woman in the chemist who suggested I look into getting my five-week-old baby's ears pinned back because, "they can fix that these days." I'm sure they can, but my child was barely out of my womb and was in her own tiny way perfect.

I ignored the fact that my life was filtered with a mask as my day was spent burdened with overwhelm. I pushed and pulled, fighting against myself. This was not how I wanted to live out my early years of motherhood. Cursing and screaming through a chasm of despair because I wasn't measuring up. But where was this measuring stick? How could I gauge whether I was in any way succeeding? It wasn't as though my kids, with their padded bums and teething rings, were judging me because I struggled to get myself and them dressed and ready to step outside the front door for a walk. They didn't care if I hadn't showered in four days, or if I was so exhausted that I left the TV on in the background and lay on the floor as they played around me (on me!).

Yet, I cared. And it seemed I was so focused on this idea of failing, that those slow, hard days were all I saw. I saw the negative. The struggle. And no possibility of change. The problem is, I was holding my imperfections in a negative light. I desperately clutched on to the paradoxical fact that one, I couldn't ask for help, and two, I couldn't do this on my own. I saw being imperfect as failing, and that everything was all my fault.

I couldn't accept that being a mother was hard, or that recovering from pregnancy and childbirth was an exhausting mess of pain and upheaval. Or that my diminishing mental health was from a chemical imbalance and not because I couldn't cope. This attempt to be perfect was very much a flaw in itself. I held my worries, my inadequacies, and my vulnerabilities tight to my chest and swaddled them for longer than either of my kids. I fought against every perceived flaw, taking the blame for every questionable decision, action, or mistake I made, when really, I should have embraced my flaws, my vulnerabilities, and talked to myself a little kinder.

Finding Fault, Or Not

Although recognizing your flaws is important, I don't want you to feel flawed. You are not at fault as you wrestle kids out of coats while kicking the oven closed on dinner, or as one arm pulls loose and your little one spins in a giggling twirl, and another kid asks you the names of the planets but all you can think of is Pluto the dog. Remember, there is only so much we can do in one single moment of motherhood, and there are far too many moments to count.

Unraveling our flaws comes with accepting who we are, making changes if necessary, and being compassionate towards ourselves. Only you will know what does or doesn't need to be changed but I want you to know that this unraveling is not a negative conversation about how we may not seem to measure up, but an important step in finally seeing ourselves so explicitly naked and raw. I do not consider my six-inch caesarean scar to be a flaw on my body, nor the cellulite expanding across my backside and down my thighs. My jagged nails and poorly plucked eyebrows are not flaws. Every part of me makes up the strong, often bewildered, caring and loving mother I am.

No one sees our flaws but us. Not really anyway. Our kids don't look at us and see that yesterday's mascara has stained our face. So, why would they notice that we battled to cook a well-balanced meal for the third day in a row. They are not judging us as harshly as we are ourselves.

What I will say to you at this point of *Unraveling Motherhood* is that to be the mother you desire to be, flaws and all, I ask you to be comfortable in your own skin, to feel confident in your choices and your capabilities, to be kind to yourself, and listen truly to what matters to you as a woman and a mother. Be the mother you see beyond the mirror.

Unraveling Self-Criticism

We are our own worst enemy half the time. At least, I know I am. The inner cogs and gears winding in my head scratch at every turn with an undulating rhythm of "nope, shouldn't have done that," and "you really think that worked?" There was a time when I would spend most of my day questioning everything I did because it turns out that when you are a mother everything you do seems to affect everyone else in your family.

When I decided not to go back to work after Devin was born, I questioned everything a hundred times over. Every time I asked a question, the guilt rose, self-doubt poured in, and crushing self-criticism gave me heart palpitations over an already stress-inducing decision. I decided to give up the daily commute and be home with the kids, but I also wanted to work. How was I going to split my time between every human in the house? I had visions of alternating my time between the then toddler who was in a very definite attachment phase, and the preschooler who equally progressed with separation anxiety. I had to fit in time with my husband which likely meant sitting on the couch with the remote between us because I also had to figure out when I would do this job I planned

Unravel

Listening to the whirlwind in our minds can be tricky. We have yet to unravel the idea that thoughts are not facts. Our difficult and self-deprecating thoughts are often our minds jumping to conclusions. Challenge any negative thoughts that creep in by asking:

- Is this true?
- Am I making assumptions?
- Am I exaggerating?
- How can I find out if what I'm thinking is true?
- Is there another way to look at it?
- How does this thought make me feel?
- What's the worst thing that can possibly happen?
- Am I 100% sure this will happen?
- Am I falling into a thinking trap?
- Am I catastrophizing?
- Am I overestimating danger?
- What would I tell a friend who thought this?

on creating for myself. Writing takes time, and head space, and is very much, in my case, a solitary experience with no distraction's mandatory. There appeared to be zero time for myself as I took a proverbial knife and dissected myself into slices to fit into a neat mental pie chart, ensuring everyone got a bite of me.

In the end, I was very much listening to that internal voice that said it cannot be done. No matter what way I looked at it, no matter how I split that pie up, I always concluded that working from home in a time-consuming job, combined with the mental load of motherhood, relationships, and the holy grail of self-care, simply could not be done.

I dumped pressure on myself. I dumped guilt. I dumped and dumped and dumped until I was in a cycle of negative self-talk.

Not only was this voice telling me I would be no good at being a journalist, but it also flat out told me that I cannot write. This inner critic was good: it knew just where to bite and hold on. I needed to talk myself out of it because I really wanted to work from home even though being a parent at the school gates challenges my introverted nature. It screamed, "what's the point of wanting to stay at home with the kids if I couldn't give them my entire attention all the time?" And this was where that biting little voice falls down.

We all have this voice in our head telling us what we should or shouldn't do. It is there to protect us, nudging us along on the safer path, and some of the time, it's a good one to listen to. There are also the times, of course, when the voice urges the already rising guilt to take over.

Pulling the Threads on Negative Self-Talk

Negative self-talk is a tricky little growly beast. It's possibly louder than most of your other thoughts because it's trying to grab your attention. Think of the 2-year-old tugging on your trouser leg, begging for a packet of Skittles, as you try to pay for groceries. It's the distraction you don't need as you dig out scrunched up coupons wedged in between year old receipts in your purse. (Q: Why do we keep so many receipts anyway? A: Because of "just in case." Everything becomes "just in case" in motherhood and chances are that "just in case" will be needed some day.)

That voice may quietly suggest, "I'm not good at this. It's better someone else does it." It may roar, "I can't do anything right at all!" It can sometimes try to be affable but offer no valid suggestions such as, "Well, that was a big old waste of time. There's no point in even trying that again," and so we give up.

Our inner critic tends not to have a filter. She blames, and judges. She picks apart your choices, decisions, catastrophes, and almost everything else, until giving up is much easier. Our self-esteem, independence, and trust in our own abilities sits on her shoulders and she so easily shakes us off. As you can imagine, it's this inner voice that stops us from making those big life changes as she knocks our confidence How is negative self-talk going to help us accept our flaws and find comfort in being good enough?

It's not. Straight up, it is one hell of a block in our road to knowing that we are doing a good job loving, protecting, caring, educating, and raising our kids. She will bite every time we question our parenting if we let her have the stage. It's not really a surprise to know that self-blame, rumination, and negative self-talk can lead to an increased risk of mental health issues such as depression, stress, and anxiety.

But why do we listen? Why do we let these inner monologues refocus our attention away from what we truly want? Quite simply, we struggle to see through the fog of the blurred emotions that rise with self-criticism. Our behaviors change because of the heightened stress, and it becomes a vicious cycle for two reasons:

Restricted thinking. The more we hear something, the more we believe it.

Perfectionism. We struggle to hit the target because our internal critic keeps moving the goalposts. Great is not good enough. Perfect is better, but we know perfect is not good enough either. Either way, we are too stressed to reach any goal and the vicious cycle continues.

Stitching Up the Idea of Negative Self-Talk

Challenging these negative thinking patterns comes with a catch. To stop them, you have to know that they are there in the first place. When we are perpetually told lies, the web of negative thinking grows bigger, thicker, and we can get very much caught up in the mess.

Recognize Your Inner Critic

We do not always pay attention to all our thoughts for a whole day. They come and go, flitting in and out of our minds the way the kids run to and from the fridge. But like the kids, they often leave a trail behind.

If the thoughts themselves are not quite recognizable, think about the feelings they conjured up. Did you notice feeling sad or anxious at any time during the day? Look for signs that you were self-critical such as gritting your teeth or chopping the carrots a little more vigorously than normal. Our actions can say a lot about what is going on in our mind.

To recognize your inner critic, ask: Can I attach this feeling to any particular thought? Does this particular thought pattern help me in any way? Is it making my life better?

Challenge Your Thoughts

If you found your thought pattern to be as useful as putting water beads in your kid's bath (10 minutes of fun, three hours of back breaking, scooping agony so no beads go down the drain), you may now recognize that you were being self-critical. It is time to challenge those thoughts.

If we let our exaggerated negative thoughts go unchallenged, they take hold and linger. The problem is that they feel real. It's in your head after all, but that's exactly why negative self-talk is a reproachful ally. There is no one there but us to tell it to shut up.

These thoughts and feelings are not reality. They are skewed ideas heavily influenced by our moods and preconceived beliefs and over-whelmed by opportune influences. So, flip the switch on your thoughts. Ask yourself are these thoughts and observations true?

My own internal voice chastises me every time I serve a "medley" plate of food for the kids' dinner. Slices of ham and salami, fresh fruit, cheese, and breadsticks. A medley is usually reserved for days when I am worn out, have brain fog or am too exhausted to stand at the stove stirring pots and mashing potatoes. A medley never feels like a "good enough" dinner. It feels like I have given up on trying to maintain a healthy balance and decided to upend the fridge instead. I could let my internal voice berate me for "failing," or I could remind myself that the kids have just about had their five-a-day, they have eaten yogurts and cereals, and will get some decent protein tomorrow when today's chicken is roasted.

Challenging our thoughts means: 1) Checking if they are real. 2) Not allowing the negative thought take hold. 3) Taking action to counter the thought.

Change Your Language

This one is a little tricky because firstly we need to recognize that we are talking down to ourselves, and we need to have the audacity to challenge it. Being bold in the face of adversity takes courage, even if we are talking to ourselves. Remember, your inner voice is not afraid to tell you that you would never get away with a red bikini after two kids (which you absolutely can by the way). Changing the words used by your inner voice can alter your internal monologue into something agreeable and healthy.

Instead of listening to intense negative language, *shift the wording to possibilities.* For example, "I can't do this," becomes, "This is a challenge I can work with." If your inner voice says, "I never get anything right," change it to, "I haven't figured this out yet." And when your voice says, "I'm not good enough," remind yourself, "I am enough. And worthy too."

Shift Your Perspective

Those ill-formed thoughts are very much part of a small internal world that negates the bigger picture. The emphasis put on them is consuming, but when we challenge that inner critic, we can shift our perspective on the situation and place those triggering thoughts out into the wider world. As the world stretches out, our unbalanced thoughts and problems become smaller, negating the fear and anxiety they may bring.

Another way to shift perspective is to ask if what you're worried about will really matter in five years? Or are you placing too great an emphasis on it?

Think Like a Friend

Would you talk to a friend the way you talk to yourself? Our inner critic can be, in three words, "a total bitch." She picks on our flaws and amplifies them until we are the worst mother ever for not letting the five-year-old sleep over at a friend's house. She twists our thoughts, exaggerating a simple error or misinterpretation of school policy to be the cause of climate change. An utterly magnified and out of proportion false thought. She criticizes us for not spending enough time with our kids, for sending them to bed early because we are all touched out, or for wanting an hour of space to scroll Instagram and watch a first dance disaster at some strangers wedding on TikTok.

She is very good at making us believe her. She is stern, harsh, and so very adamant that we listen as she pulls on our trouser leg spitting those Skittles at us. We listen because she lives in our head. But ask yourself if what she says is justifiable? Would you talk to a friend the same way you talk to yourself? Would you reprimand and punish her, make her feel guilty, unworthy, or wrong? If you know you would not talk to a friend this way, shift the way you speak to yourself.

#Motherhood

I am all for being honest about the perfect storm of parenting. Especially when I am so overwhelmed that I want to run out of the house, or when dizzy spells hit because I have not slept in three nights, and especially when I want to lock myself in the bathroom with a packet of crisps. If only everyone recognized that it is perfectly okay to feel the weight of the hard moments, and that #motherhood is not a competition or in any way perfect. Maybe then, we wouldn't feel so bad about a camera reel with snaps of scrunched-up crying eyes or bored, tired faces after a failed family day out. Real life happens beyond our screens. Perfect is not a word you need to be concerned about when you are a parent. "Good enough" is what we need to aim for and trust me, you are already there.

It is very easy to get caught up in the competitive nature of motherhood. To balance our life against someone else and feel flawed or pick at our supposed weaknesses. But we are not weak, or flawed, or broken. We are learning and growing and embracing who we are. To unravel this idea, be kind to yourself, forgive yourself, and learn to laugh when you make mistakes.

Be Kind to Yourself

We can spend our time berating ourselves for what we should or could have done differently. Or we can learn from our mistakes, be kind to ourselves, and recognize we have limitations. We are a work in progress and that is a wonderful thing.

Forgive Yourself

There are things we can change or at least focus on to help shift our internal monologue of guilt when we feel as though we have made a mistake. Shouting at the kids because of frustration and anxiety was something I felt inherently flawed on. I saw it as a weakness within a spiraling emotional despair. It took me two years to control that anger and another two to forgive myself for it.

There are things about us that we cannot change. It is not exactly easy to accept these faults, so what I will ask of you is to look at *why* you see something as a flaw or a weakness. Is something blocking you from forgiving yourself?

Learn To Laugh at Yourself

Laughter, the greatest stress reliever, the ultimate release. Combating that negative thought pattern connected to our flawed human nature can be unraveled by learning to laugh at ourselves.

chapter 5

Unraveling Control

● **Control** \ kən -ˈtrōl \
**To direct the behavior of (a person or animal): to cause
(a person or animal) to do what you want**
Dictionary, **Merriam-Webster**

FOR A LONG TIME, I looked through an opaque window on my life and saw a woman very much in control of not only herself, but all that was around her. This was a woman who created a new persona for herself with her distinguishable buzzcut, who spoke so freely on social media about the challenges of life as a mother. A woman who oozed all sorts of perceived power and control over her home, which she kept ordered and organized, with her kids who were polite and well-behaved in adult company. A woman so in control of her destiny that she created and explored a lifetime passion and turned it into a job during a time of ailing mental health.

But as I say, this window was opaque. It was tinted with the sticky fingerprints, thick dust, and chocolate mud of regular living. So, it did not give a particularly clear image of what day-to-day living was really like and how utterly out of control I actually was. From the outside, anyone looking at my life may have believed I was a centered, strong, and dependable mother who found mindfulness, meditation, and a muddled calm. A woman most certainly in control. In some ways, yes, I had a god-like grip on varying aspects of my life, those things which benefit from a firm level of control, such as managing the taxes and bringing the bins out in time for the binmen to haul away the debris of a busy household. However, if you were to spray a bit of Windolene onto that glass, you would see the cracks, the scratches, and the threatening fracture lines.

That undulating need to be physically, mentally, and overbearingly in control, to have perplexing power over certain elements of my life, was not a good thing and was definitely out of character. I desperately needed control, to the point of having anxiety and panic attacks if I, in any way, did not have a handle on the minute details of life with toddlers and preschoolers. This need for control was not a good thing. It created a false security. There was no satisfaction or relief, no comfort because for every moment I had perceived control, the more I needed. It was a vice holding me together in a most peculiar way as anxiety built these desperate attempts to control and conquer motherhood. It created tight knots in need of distinctive loosening.

That need for stability was uncontrollable at times (ironic, I know) and led to an inevitable overwhelm as I structured not only my day but that of my kids and Barry, including their behaviors, actions, and voices at times. I controlled in a way that was negative, unhelpful, and certainly unhealthy for all of us, but the idea of letting go of this newfound and difficult to hold on to control was ultimately terrifying for me. I had lost all semblance of power over my thoughts, my actions, my ideas, my dreams, my future, and without controlling my day-to-day life, including those who lived it with me, I was powerless, failing, struggling.

Control was a part of my unraveling that I, firstly, didn't recognize until I began to closely look at those behaviors which grated against my natural instincts; and secondly, actively ignored because, well, it was a somewhat uncomfortable by-product of my struggle with anxiety. Being in control was a power I needed to feel secure in my motherhood and in my head.

This need for safety as a coping mechanism is a complicated aspect of our lives to unravel. Our relationship with control can be a good thing. It can also be somewhat complex. It goes without saying that severe control issues are a problem and need to be tackled with a professional. However, throughout this chapter, we are not unraveling the idea of the "controlling mother," which is seen as the use of psychological and manipulative control to influence our children's behavior, or parental authority. That is a somewhat different and varied concept based on the unique influences that behavioral and psychological control have on our children's development. That knot is heavily outside of my authority to discuss and is a different construct to our internal unraveling of control that dictates how we can manage and maintain the overwhelm of motherhood.

These questions about "the controlling mother" are, of course, subjects worth investigating for ourselves as we parent our children into adulthood. Our actions as over-protective, controlling, and overbearing parents, otherwise known as helicopter parenting, as we anxiously hover around our kids, are proven to have a distinctive effect on our children, their traits, and the type of person they will grow up to be. However, researchers investigating the relationship between helicopter parenting and children's development have found mixed results.[1] For instance, we may automatically believe that being a controlling parent is a bad thing leading to distress, loss of autonomy, feelings of incompetence, and decreased self-esteem. But studies have also found that adolescents with controlling parents report a positive parent-adolescent relationship and can be associated with positive self-esteem and self-efficacy.[2]

So, let's preface this conversation with the knowledge that control is not necessarily the evil we assume it to be. When we begin to realize that we are attempting to control our lives, and possibly the lives of those around us, in an untoward manner, that's when things get problematic. We do not set out to become controlling or have that overwhelming need to be in control, so we have to remember that a lot of these power struggles in motherhood are part of our human nature. We naturally gravitate towards controlling that which puts our family and us at risk, causes discomfort in our lives, or threatens to destabilize our finally found equilibrium.[3]

Even so, that age-old tome of guilt may sit heavy in our hands when we realize our behaviors are reactionary, unnecessary, and somewhat knotted. This is why I want you to remember that throughout all of this, you are still unraveling, stitching up, and unraveling again. Control is a complicated pattern to follow.

What we are unknotting here is that intricate balance between what we do and do not have control over, an unknotting of unconscious control as we attempt to align our values, our needs, and our way of living to that which we believe is our truth. Remember that this chapter is not a trigger for the portrayal of the controlling mother.

What Is Control?

I didn't start off this unraveling, asking myself, "Am I a controlling person?" In fact, the word control never even came into my mind. Instead, I asked myself, in a roundabout sort of way, "Why do I need everything to be just so?"

Why did I have to have the baby bag packed exactly how I needed it. And why if Barry put the Sudocrem in the wrong pocket did I snap at him? Why did I expect him to know the military precision of how I packed a baby bag with the right number of nappy sacks, a packet and a half of wipes, three nappies, and a change of clothes folded in the right way (onesie, vest, and cardigan rolled together with one sock on each end holding it all together like a perfect non-creasing package) all neatly positioned in the right order?

Why did I feel anxious if my baby did not drink the "right" amount of formula for her feeds, especially the last bottle before bed? Why was it important to abide by my rule of "everything in its place?" Why would I get upset if the toaster wasn't neatly packed away after it was used? Why did I stop Barry mid-sentence and not allow him to finish his thought because I wasn't comfortable with what he was saying or how he was saying it? Why did I try to control his way of parenting when it didn't match up with mine?

Why was I strict on bedtimes to the minute, or fight with the kids to empty their plates when they weren't hungry, or vacuum every single day, sometimes two or three times? Why, when I grew comfortable in motherhood, did I uncomfortably try to take over when I was not the one in control of a situation? Why did I think I was the only one who could fix the kids' homework anxiety or calm the toddler mid-tantrum? Why did I think my way was more compassionate and caring than anyone else's?

Why could I not go with the flow of the ordinary, chaotic life of motherhood? Where did this need for power come from?

Unraveling control is so deeply embedded in a psychological construct that any of us would struggle to understand and console our relationship with it, especially when it is so volatile at times and takes us away from our true self.

I enlisted the support of chartered counselling psychologist, Aisling Leonard-Curtin, to help make some sense of this desire and need to be in control. I came to know Aisling through my work as a journalist and connected with her positivity and belief in the good of people. Aisling radiates warmth, encouragement, and optimism, and I hang on her every word. I first approached her a few years back for insight on *The Bald Truth About Why I Shaved My Head,* an article I wrote for the Irish

Examiner in the beginning of my freelance writing career and a few months after the buzz.

Her insight on why our idea of how a woman should look remains inherently tied to the preferred feminine, struck a chord with me on how we understand and navigate our need for control. She said, "It is more helpful when each woman gives herself a chance to *choose* what is *authentic* for her in any given context and be open to this *changing* in different contexts and at different times in her life. We will not be able to *escape* our earlier life experiences and the many *internalized comments* we have heard. However, we can *actively* make choices in the *present* moment that can bring us closer towards more authentically *living* our lives."[4]

The connection between choosing, living authentically, making changes, the need for escape, the internalized comments, and actively living in the present, highlights so much about how control obscures many other aspects of our lives and blocks us from living authentically. As we aim to control our environment, we are not making active choices that will support us in the long run, we are not living in a way that is true to us, we are stuck and avoid the change that is so inherently needed in this transition to motherhood. Yet, we are also trying to escape that change while being led by the internal monologue that fear spits out, and we are most certainly not living in the present. As Aisling said to me as she helped me unravel this concept, we need to look at the costs and benefits of this level of control.

The funny thing about control is that it is often a protective shield we carry to nurture our mental wellbeing. It improves our health, activity patterns, mood, and sociability. However, this can be a "perceived control" or an "illusion of control" as we become quite embedded with dictating our motherhood as we risk assess and manage every moment of our lives. Perceived control refers to our belief about our own capability of exerting influence on internal states and behaviors, as well as our external environment.[5] Whereas the illusion of control overestimates how much control we actually have.

The transition into motherhood without unraveling can leave us out of control, spinning, trying to catch a loose thread. Whatever grasp we had on our days was slowly (or quickly) loosening, so we clutch and grab at anything that will keep us steady. We lean towards control in an attempt to alleviate anxiety, stress, and loss of power. However, we may become consumed by the need to live a predictable, safe, and controlled week, hour by hour, meaning, we may struggle to respond well to anything being out of control. Because we struggle to see the paradox of control; we keep on trying. Added to that, because motherhood is wildly ambiguous, the trying gets harder with less and less return.

Control and the Uncertainty of Motherhood

A great deal of uncertainty comes with motherhood. It is quite a fragile state of being as someone who determines how the overall chaos of our lives pans out with kids, and I mean chaos in the nicest way possible. It is an upheaval with intense dynamic shifts which leave us somewhat confused as to how to manage the multiple needs of multiple people, especially when you only have two hands and one unraveling mind. It is no wonder that we may fall into a system with routinely intensifying power struggles, and not always external battles such as making sure the kids do not eat food off the supermarket floor. Internal conflicts encourage us to second-guess ourselves or blame ourselves for someone else's questionable choices.

Power and control exist in all of our relationships. We make choices and have the ability to influence not only our homes and working lives, but also those around us. It gives us the necessary natural control to exert our power so that our needs are met in the most appropriate way, even more so when we are a mother as our ultimate aim is to support and nurture our family. Control almost naturally becomes part of our protective nature in motherhood, consciously or not.

Yet, we may notice the effect that this power has on us when those anxious thoughts, worries, and fears are challenged as we curl our fingers around that necessity to control. We become effective in managing our day and our emotions, and in calming that inner turmoil that tries to tell us that we are losing the ability to keep everything under control. When anxiety builds, I clean, tidy, or organize in order to exert some level of power over my environment. Order over chaos. Tidy over messy. Quiet over loud. I make the choices, and my family follows suit because my behavior dictates that they listen and follow my lead. As though clearing away the dust bunnies will relieve the stress and overwhelm sitting under my fingernails. Or that silencing a loud house and hiding the obnoxiously noisy toys will slow my breathing and loosen my shoulders. The more I control, the more I need to control, and it becomes an addiction of sorts embedded with that fear of being out of control.

The belief that I was in control of my environment made me trust that I had power over my situation. The more control I had, the less stress I felt, and suddenly things were no longer happening "to" me but because of me. However, this was another knot to unravel in the pattern of my mental health, because, while there are always elements of our lives we can control, there are plenty of others we cannot.

My controlling behavior spread out as far as I could manage, but I was oblivious to the fact that there were plenty of situations where I did not have that perceived power, and so the knot tightened as I controlled deeper, harder, and often more desperately. Ultimately, I made my life and my family's life so tightly knotted as I veered into attempting to control every aspect, much of which I should have had no authority over.

There comes a time, though, when our behaviors may be highlighted to us by others, or we may recognize our own tendencies to act out of character. As such, my unraveling began early when my mother and sister recognized anger and control shuffled to the forefront of my manners. By them holding the threads for me, I could notice a shift in my thought patterns. However, I did not change at this stage. It was only the beginning. Over the next three years, anxiety continued to warp my mind, and the need for control deepened. It took a long time for me to question what I believed I had control over during those heightened periods of long-lasting anxiety and how I viewed my parenting efforts.

The only way for me to actively view this behavior was to wipe clean that window until it was sparkling and clearly look at what I was trying to control, why I tried to control it, and whether I truly needed to control it. These questions were not a happy intrusion because I didn't like what I saw. As I say, the guilt struck heavily when I saw how my actions affected those I loved most. So, I asked myself, what could I let go of for a calmer way of living, to increase my confidence, self-efficacy, and for stronger emotional health? Letting go of certain struggles is to gain greater power.

Unravel

Aisling says, "When faced with uncertainty, we often treat it as a problem. It can be tempting and desirable to try to resolve uncertainty and kick ourselves into action to answer all our questions. However, while this is entirely normal and natural, doing so can bring us further away from who and where we want to be. While avoiding or jumping to resolve uncertainty immediately can feel good in the short term, it almost inevitably results in us feeling worse in the long term and further away from our values."

As a mother, can you recognize times when you weren't open to sitting with uncertainty? This could be something about your child's health, their wellbeing, where they will go to school or where you will live.

When we consider balancing our understanding of control, we can ask ourselves questions such as, did I rush to make the uncertain certain? What kind of things did I start or stop doing when I wasn't open to uncertainty? What were the benefits of that in the short term? And were there any costs to not sitting with this uncertainty?

What question or uncertainty arose in your mind?

_____

_____

_____

What thoughts or emotions did you feel?

_____

_____

_____

What bodily sensations did you feel?

_____

_____

_____

What benefits or costs did you experience?

_____

_____

_____

Locus of Control

Let's take a quick step back and look at locus of control because it was a factor that helped me unknot my reasonings for not only needing control but recognizing the power I have as a mother and a woman.

The "locus of control" pertains to the degree in which we believe that the outcomes we work towards are either a result of our own behaviors, or from external forces that have a greater influence than we do over the results.

Introduced into psychology in 1966 by Julian Rotter, an internal locus of control points to believing that we are in charge of our destiny and have control over our success.[6] It means we are more likely to take responsibility for our actions, we are less influenced by others, have a strong sense of self-efficacy, meaning we believe in ourselves, we feel confident in taking on challenges, and are noted as being happier and more fulfilled in our work and home life.

Traditionally, studies suggest an external locus of control is ordinarily identified in those of us with depression or anxiety disorders, and a belief that we have no control over our destiny.[7] Yet, I veered heavily into believing that I had control over everything. I was led by a fear that I had no control over anything and pushed to prove that fear wrong.

On the flip side, the external locus of control supposes that outside forces, even luck or chance, have a greater effect on our level of success. We blame others, are easily influenced, feel stuck in our situation with no change on the horizon, and feel helpless or powerless.

Locus of control, however, is a momentum, and neither is explicitly good or bad. Where we sit on the spectrum of control moves and alters depending on where we are in life, with most of us gravitating towards one or the other throughout our lives. It is not necessarily a stagnant force and can shift and merge and expand throughout our lives depending on how we respond to major changes in our environment and how we perceive our level of control. It is more difficult to lean closer to an internal locus of control when we have long lived by an external locus of control.

As parents, our locus of control has been associated with our children's outcomes which suggests that changing from an external locus of control would be beneficial and worthwhile before we even enter parenthood. It is worthwhile to recognize our thought patterns and connect them to how we make decisions, what we do, and what happens as a result. Understanding if we have an internal or external locus of control and shifting appropriately will not only benefit us but also our children.[8]

For about two years after Devin was born, my mental capacity convinced me that I had control over almost everything in my life. I was empowered by this internal energy to ensure everything went as it should. I made the decisions; everything came down to me.

But in truth, I was battered by an internal versus external mentality as I blamed everything on myself and worked harder and harder at maintaining control over absolutely everything, even the worldwide tangents I clearly had zero control over. Ultimately, I tried to fix everything myself because I was trying to fix and control my internal mind (which I have since learned did not need fixing and was not broken).

The overwhelm of taking on all the responsibility of parenthood is simply ridiculous. It aggravated my already knotted anxiety, stress, fear, and worries a hundred-fold. When it comes to motherhood, it can feel as though much of what we struggle with is out of our hands, so we may inherently and unconsciously find replacements to deliver that sense of control back into our lives.

If I felt things beginning to spiral out of control, I shifted to manage something I did have power over. However, that need for control amplified and intensified as uncontrollable life situations took over. Unchecked, that need can verge into much deeper territory outside of needing a strictly organized home as we may try to control and have power over not only situations but those around us.

So, where did I feel my locus of control sat? Was it internal? Did I truly have control over my life? Was it external? Did I think I was incapable of managing the spiraling anxiety? Was there nothing I could do? I was in yet another state of flux as I battered between the two. How do we unravel such a complicated knot?

Unravel

Think about the following statements:

- I feel like I have little control over my life.
- I don't think people get what they deserve.
- I don't bother setting goals or making plans because I don't know what might happen.
- Life is all about chance and luck.
- We don't have much influence over what happens in the world.

Agreeing or identifying with any of the above statements may indicate you have an external locus of control.

- Hard work and commitment mean I can achieve anything I set my mind too.
- I don't believe in fate or destiny.
- Being prepared, studying, and working hard will pay off.
- Success is about dedication and effort.
- We get what we deserve in life.

Agreeing or identifying with any of the above statements may indicate you have an internal locus of control.

The Control Paradox

It is very easy to live within an illusion of control as I did. We overestimate how much control we actually have and actively work at managing the uncontrollable. Of course, when we see results, we think we played a hand in the outcome, but are we really in control, or are we looking for that perceived control to manage the underlying need to feel in control?

The thing about control is that I had very little. Beneath it all, I lived with fear and uncertainty. My response was to take over any given situation as much as possible to make sure I, and my family, were as safe, supported, comfortable, and as happy as possible. It was led by the fear and anxiety that came with being out of control, of having unrealistic expectations of what life as a mother was like, and a lack of confidence as a parent. It is well researched that those of us who have perceived control experience more positive emotion and increased motivation which supports our mental wellbeing. This is because we avoid the negative consequences of being out of control which allows us to take credit for successful actions.[9]

But the truth is, we cannot control everything and nor should we want to. The variety and spontaneity of life can be somewhat special.

We cannot control what other people say, do, or think. We cannot control their emotions, their thoughts, or who they are friends with. We have no say in what they think of our children or us, and we cannot make them change. We have no power over the weather, worldwide events, and cannot turn the traffic lights from red to green by blinking, or change the bus timetable, the school calendar, or the overtime hours of our partner.

We may dwell on our disappointments and regrets, ruminating over past events because we think we should have been able to control them. The more we try to manage the multiple facets of our lives, the greater risk we will take in gaining that control.

Living under the illusion of control affects not only our own mindset, but the lives of those closest to us who are directly impacted by our attempts to control. Micromanaging our children's lives, our own, and that of our partners has a consequence on the entire family dynamic. Not only will we exhaust ourselves, but we are taking decisions, autonomy, and independence away from those we care for most. We teach our little ones that if we do not have control over everything, something will go wrong. As we fear our own mistakes, our kids begin to fear theirs instead of taking responsibility and learning through the blunders that happen in life.

Our lives can feel as though they are spinning out of control as we try our absolute best to mother in the only way we know how to. The responsibility and feeling of expectation is enormous, but our realization comes when we respect the fact that we are one solitary human being who is intrinsically human.

While this illusion of control can make us feel temporarily more motivated, better about ourselves, and impacts our overall health, it is a significantly false sense of control that cannot be maintained long term. We may struggle to learn from our mistakes and suffer intense self-criticism, blame, and guilt.

When it comes to learning what we can control, we have to look internally. We may not have explicit control over our world, but we do have power over our reactions. How we respond to situations that are out of our control is the ultimate knot that leads to unraveling control.

Unravel

What You Have Control Over	What You Don't Have Control Over
How you respond and act	How others react, respond, act
Your boundaries	How others behave
What you focus on	Other people's mistakes
Your habits	Others' opinions of you
How you spend your time	The past and the future
How you speak to yourself and others	How others feel
Setting goals and working towards them	Getting someone to change
Choosing to love yourself	When others are negative
Finding purpose in life	If others accept you
How we respond to unwanted thoughts, emotions, uncertainties, and challenges	

Control in Motherhood

With motherhood comes uncertainty, anxiety, stress, and possible insecurity. Life is in a state of instability as we gather the multicolored Magna Tiles stuck to the fridge, the Hevesh5 neon dominos sprawled on the kitchen floor, and the loose red and blue pieces from Connect4 in all four corners of the house. We count them one by one and find comfort in knowing we have all the parts together, safely packed away in their correct boxes.

Slowly but surely, this behavior of finding the right place, having everything where it belongs, and being in control of even small aspects of our busy and complicated lives becomes a relief. The controlling behavior that we are unraveling comes unconsciously into our lives, often as a result of anxiety, fear, or insecurity. We do simple things to adjust our sense of safety.

Through my own unraveling, the knots of my need for control have proven to be rigid and limitless. The more control I had, the more I needed, and as such, the tighter I held on to that perceived power. Anxiety is a perplexing conundrum our minds attempt to fix in whatever manner it can. For me, it was that need for a secure, understood, and predictable space against the anxiety that rattled in my mind and body. Control was a calming presence, and it was easier to step in when things momentarily went askew to regain that balance.

I aimed to control:

How clean my home was. From the fingerprints on the window, the grease in the cooker, the dust along the skirting board, the toys on the floor, to making sure everything sat at a perfect angle in the correct spot. But what control do we really have when we are not the only ones messing up a house? It is near impossible to continually keep a clean and tidy home, yet I worked damn hard to achieve it because controlling the dirt in my home was a replacement for my lack of control over the thoughts and fears in my head.

Our daily routine. Routines are by and large uncontrollable, especially when kids are small. There is always a plan B, C, and D, but I did my level best to rely on plan A. It was when my two were babies and toddlers that I veered so heavily into a need to control our daily life down to the timings of meals because there were appointments to be made, school runs to be done, and bedtime struggles to overcome. Missing the mark on any of these and the other 324 events that needed monitoring and controlling in our lives meant I wasn't in control.

Behaviors—mine, theirs, and his. If an argument was on the horizon, my anxiety-ridden body could not handle the aggro, the enhanced emotions, the biting words. So, I attempted to quell it before it became an issue, as though I had a say in whether someone in our household was allowed to be angry, sad, frustrated, or excited. Controlling the attitudes, actions, and emotions of others is not only not possible but not necessary or right.

How other people see me. For a while, buzzing my head, tattooing my arm, and smiling on Instagram was enough to portray an image of myself as being whole-heartedly empowered and in control of my life, my mothering, my mental health. It didn't take long, of course, for me to believe that I needed to do more to prove myself to others and control not only how they saw me but what they thought of me. My social feeds became curated, which didn't always reflect the reality of my life, but it meant I was sharing what I had control over. The problem with this was that my need to be a certain kind of person online was not about control but being controlled by the media mill, which played havoc with how I saw myself, taunting my values and aspirations in life.

The need for control in motherhood can come down to many different things, including our mental health, our confidence, and this state of unstable, varying change. Recognizing and identifying what may be the cause is not as simple as ticking a box but a deep and inner exploration of the many knots in our lives.

Potential explanations for needed control include:

- Stress or anxiety
- Fear of failure
- Fear of losing control
- Perfectionism
- Fear of abandonment
- Fear of being hurt
- Being highly sensitive
- An absence of trust
- Low or damaged self-esteem
- Traumatic life experiences
- Past experiences of controlling behavior

Our level of control becomes questionably compromised when it is almost handed over to our newborn, who unknowingly dictates our lives from when we eat to how many hours of sleep we manage to tot up in a night. As we give our all to care, love, and nurture our children, our power is diverted. Added to this is the expectation of motherhood, and when it does not match with what we expect, we can feel helpless and powerless.

Over time, we learn how to challenge that control and bring back a sense of balance as those newborn days end. It then becomes about recognizing and realizing we have unrealistic control expectancies and figuring out if we are living under an illusion of control.

Unravel

Think about the following statements:

- Am I a perfectionist?

- Do I try to please everyone?

- Do I criticize others?

- Is everything black and white to me? Am I inflexible?

- Do I have a hard time letting go of mistakes, fears, or worries?

- Do I struggle to accept when I'm wrong?

Loosening Small Knots

How do we let go of control and allow ourselves to be vulnerable? I have always had a tendency to plan and organize to a level that manifested in a way I believed was right. But these were usually things I had power over, such as our itinerary on holiday. A well-planned day is an exhausting but fulfilled day, but I was always open to situations, to unavoidable closures, and that Plan B. I was able and willing to let go when and if necessary. However, enter motherhood and letting go was not on the cards and Plan B was not preferable. This was something I had to learn, grow with, and essentially become comfortable with again.

Letting go may mean less control, but it also means more spontaneity, less stress, less indecision, more connection, greater support, and overall, a slowing down. It means opening ourselves to greater possibilities as we share choices, take an unknown path, and embrace being open to challenges. We can be in control of our lives without attempting to pigeonhole every aspect into what we need to be on the right path. That need for control is led by the fear of the unknown, but the unknown can be exciting, encouraging, and liberating.

We have knotted up our lives by believing we can dictate and direct so much of what we do. But we can unknot much of it by focusing on why we feel the urge to control and questioning whether there is any real control in the first place.

Reassess What You Can Control

We all have goals in life. These goals may have become obscured, forgotten, or loosely wound up in the knots of other aspects of our lives, so we may need to work through what exactly they are again. They are the things we can focus on to move forward in our lives and whether they are in or out of our control. Understanding our goals again can help us reassess what we control by asking, "What do I want from my life?"

Make a list of your goals. It could be a short list, and it could grow longer than you imagine. These are the things in life you want to achieve. Now, looking at your list, pinpoint your strengths and assess whether you have control over these goals. What can you do to reach them? And what may be out of your control

Knowing our goals and whether we have the ability to make a plan of action to reach these goals helps us to be aware of the elements of our life that we do have control over.

Shift Your Mindset

I seem to be all about mindset, but I do believe that how we think is a large knot in the thread or a giant coffee spill on the pattern. Listening to our thoughts influences our reactions and responses. When it comes to control, if something doesn't go as planned, we criticize ourselves, place blame on our shoulders, and struggle to learn from our mistakes.

By shifting our mindset, instead of taking that responsibility as a fault, we can find compassion and learn that we are ever-changing, constantly unraveling individuals. We may realize that we never had implicit control over the situation, that we could not have changed the outcome, or that perhaps we could do something differently next time.

Look For a New Perspective

Our control is deeply embedded in a belief that we can and should do it all by ourselves. It is expected of us, and what we often expect of ourselves. Until we realize that this is not true, the expectation of motherhood is difficult to unravel. We are often living in the future as expectations compound our vision. We control as much as we can so that we keep ourselves safe from disappointment, fear, and supposed failure. Living in the future will not help us in any scenario, so focus on grounding. Root yourself in the present moment and build your trust in yourself. The more respect, trust, and self-worth you have, the greater your ability to let go of that need to control will be.

Unravel

Write down a fear list. Not exactly the easiest unraveling exercise considering we tend to run away from our fears, or not attribute our behaviors to a feeling of fear. Our fears, however, have a big impact on us. They dictate our actions, our thoughts, our movement in life. They can act as blocks, stopping us from moving forward. By actively recognizing our fears and challenging them, we give ourselves the opportunity to grow in confidence, and take back our power from that which holds us back. What's on your list?

_____

_____

_____

The Power of Small

"While you may not be capable of controlling all aspects of your life, you do have it within you to change the areas where you are giving your power away needlessly," says Aisling and Trish Leonard-Curtin in their book *The Power of Small*, which is a liberating read for those of us aiming to take action but daunted by the steps ahead of us.[10] The books tag line pretty much sums up what we need in life: "making tiny but powerful changes when everything feels too much."

"What type of parent would you choose to be if you could choose?" Aisling asked me, which in all honesty, stumped me because of its entirely complex answer. Could I actually choose? "Control is about deciphering what way you want to respond to those choices?" she says, "What type of life do you want to choose? Often it is more empowering to think about the kinds of qualities we wish to bring to bear in terms of parenting in this uncertain uncontrollable world. And also remember that it is impossible to be a perfect parent or person. It's also impossible to live in line with our values one hundred percent of the time, so part of it is about having a solid anchor and guide and returning to our idea of parenthood over time."

Throwing it all down on paper, I came up with keywords to unravel my idea of choosing how I would ideally parent. I would be supportive, kind, energetic. I would carve out time specifically for each child, explore worlds, old and new, with them both, give them all my attention and never be pulled away, distracted, or absent-minded. I would be entertaining, fun, creative, and dynamic. I would educate and nurture. I then imagine I would be exhausted, overwhelmed, overworked, and resentful. So, I shift my idea of motherhood to include what I am capable of. All I can think of is that I would be there. I would be there emotionally, physically, and spiritually. If this was the type of parent I wanted to be, how come I did not unravel this against control when I fell so eloquently into recognizing that I was flawed and human?

The answer is simple yet complex. While being flawed allowed me to make mistakes, my natural instinct to protect was embedded in control which remained knotted because of the fear attached to anxiety. While I was beginning to accept my nature as a flawed mother, I did not recognize that I was in a power struggle and was not making the right moves, those small steps, to let go.

"There are always benefits to control. If there weren't benefits, we wouldn't do it," Aisling tells me. "Generally, when we engage in controlling behaviors or actions, we usually get to feel something that we want to feel in the short term or feel less of something we don't want to feel. It can often help us to feel more in control or more empowered, even if that's not necessarily the case. The cost of this control may actually take away from the very thing that we want to have, like the kind of connected relationships we want to have with our children or with others."

When we realize that power over certain situations in life is out of our control, we can learn to adapt. How we respond to this experience, in a way paradoxically, gives us some power back. For instance, certain conversations were off the table for a long time for me, such as Devin's incredibly poor sleeping habits overnight. She was one of those toddlers who wouldn't let you out of the room, so I would cramp up on a small chair in her bedroom with a thin blanket over me willing her to sleep, but those three-hour waking's at 2am were out of my control. Sometimes, because I stayed cramped on that chair, comforting her, I felt in control (It took two years for me to accept help and share the load with Barry). In the meantime, when Barry attempted to discuss sleep training or after any mention of her achingly painful sleep habits, I shut down, silenced him, actively ignored his support because I took his commentary as blame on me or blame on Devin, who I was incredibly protective over. Ignoring the outside influences outside of my exhausted, red-eyed bubble meant I was not controlling the situation. There was zero control in this situation and adverse implications as a result of my behavior. I was upsetting Barry, and our relationship was negatively affected partly due to my reactions.

In many instances of my motherhood life, my need for control was, in fact, a reaction to avoiding an outcome I didn't want. Barking orders at the kids—shoes, coat, hat, brush your teeth, eat, sit still, turn that off—were all a manner of reflecting my control on a situation so that I felt in balance but were often not necessary.

Aisling explains the importance of recognizing the motivation between having "more control" or "more meaning" while remembering that not all control is bad. We sometimes think that the more we try to control, the more we get it, but the paradox is that the more we try to get control the harder it is. "It's worth questioning," she says, "why you want to move closer towards meaning and engaging in more toward moves in the here and now. A *toward* move is any action where the primary motivation helps you move closer toward who you are and where you want to be as a parent and as a person. And an *away* move is any action that's primarily motivated by trying to get away from something that you don't want to think or feel or an outcome that you don't want to have. We're not saying all away moves are bad, but it's about recognizing how often am I engaging in toward moves and how often am I engaging in away moves and is this working for myself as a parent and in my life in general?"

We can find ourselves stuck in a pattern of control. We may be unmindful of our actions, we may not understand what is most important to us at the moment, or we may not connect our actions to our values and beliefs and instead, react due to emotions or thoughts and vulnerabilities. In this way, we may be reacting in a manner that means we are reducing, avoiding, or limiting our experiences to protect ourselves. Essentially, we pull away from being our true selves.

"Taking small manageable steps towards empowerment," says Aisling, "can take us outside of our comfort zone but within our self-care zone that will bring us closer towards meaning and closer towards being the kind of parent and person that we want to be. This can be reaching out and asking for help, taking more time for self-care or something that actively benefits you."

Unravel

Again, tune in to how much of your time and energy is being wasted trying to control the aspects of your life that are essentially out of your control.

What type of parent would you choose if you could choose? What are the qualities you wish to embody as a parent?

_____

_____

_____

What are your toward moves? What are the actions that bring you closer to being this type of parent?

_____

_____

_____

What do you want to control, avoid, or get rid of in the realms of motherhood

_____

_____

_____

What are your away moves, those actions you engage in to move away from your vulnerabilities as a mother?

_____

_____

_____

The Controllable Nature of Motherhood

Mothering is a power struggle at the best of times. There are a million small wins and an exponential number of losses on a Monday. By Friday, it has flipped to more winning. It is volatile. Explorative. Exhausting. Mentally draining. It is no wonder that we hold on tightly to anything that encourages some semblance of control. Life is fundamentally unpredictable, and when we are stuck in a circle of control, we can forget this simple fact. Life with children adds another loop to the rollercoaster.

In this entire narrative of control, I want you to know that you are not the only one to have felt these feelings of a constant need for control as we try to offset the uncontrollable imbalance of actions we cannot fully account for. Because it feels as though we are the only one white-knuckled on the ride, we can easily withdraw or isolate ourselves as we unravel. Letting go and feeling out of control is quite simply not a nice feeling. It is at times like these that we need friends and family more than ever to ground us, stabilize us, or even hold us up temporarily as we come off the ride dizzy and nauseous. With their support, we can learn to control our reactions to the things that are well out of our control.

When we can't control what is happening, we can challenge how we respond to that lack of control. So, while everything can feel uncontrollable, I want to remind you:

Every Feeling is Valid

Our feelings are there for a reason. We may not like that reason, but being honest about what is happening for us, without judgement, will give us the opportunity to heal from those feelings. We may try to run away and hide from the strong emotions that rock us, but by giving ourselves permission to feel those rising sentiments, naming them and acknowledging them, we grow and learn.

Remember to Breathe

Breathe and be conscious of your breath. Overwhelm, fear, panic can make us lose our focus on our breath. In fact, many of us are not conscious of our breath, despite it being a vital force. Quick, shallow breathing is a bodily response as our stress levels elevate. We find that we cannot think, our body shuts down, and we ultimately lose all control. Breathe.

chapter 6

Unraveling Boundaries

Boundary \ baủn-d(ə-)rē \
something that indicates or fixes a limit or extent
Dictionary, **Merriam-Webster**

S ET BOUNDARIES. LEARN TO say no. Hold your own space. These
are things I have heard repeatedly since I started scrolling through
motherhood boards and Instagram, attempting to validate my feelings
and experiences through memes, journal prompts, and inspirational
quotes. Of course, I found extraordinarily little support in there, but
rather, a heap of woulds, coulds, and shoulds, which tightened the knots
of my motherhood even more. The problem with encouraging words
online is that they float in front of us as simply that—words, displayed
in a pretty font, sitting on an image of a frosty woodland or shimmering
lake telling us that "Boundaries are healthy, normal, and necessary" or
"Your current safe boundaries were once unknown frontiers." Words
with little meaning, understanding, or structure to help us actively work
through elements of our life.

For me, the idea of setting boundaries meant nothing more than
building a fence or planting hedging around my house. Boundary lines

were drawn with thick black marker and were visible, quantifiable. Not imaginary musings that I couldn't maintain. Personal space only became an issue for me as my kids grew bigger and bolder and almost everything was suddenly pushed in front of my face as children have absolutely no concept of why such close proximity is frustrating. Saying no was not an active thought but a response to availability, with a side order of guilt.

When it came to personal boundaries in motherhood, I was not aware that they came in the form of physical boundaries, emotional boundaries, time, thoughts, relationships, and even our curiosity. I didn't realize I could hold boundaries with myself *and* give myself permission to reparent myself.

In fact, boundaries in general seemed to disappear with motherhood as I became almost owned by so many around me—by my children; my husband; relatives who wanted to see the babies regardless of whether I was emotionally or physically available; schools who needed support, time, and effort from the available parent; playdates; the house; the boss; the neighborhood watch. Saying no became obscured as I grew into being always accessible and responsible.

We become a focal point for so many others in motherhood, regardless of our internal mind becoming almost immediately exhausted, knotted, and heavily occupied with things outside of our control. Is it any wonder that we feel the need to strengthen our defenses when our boundaries—our physical, social, emotional, mental, and spiritual limitations—face tremendous pressure?

Because we are practically thrown into motherhood, we do not have the time or head space to figure out how to set boundaries; or why we even need them. Having no distinct understanding of the boundaries I needed and feeling guilty when I had a vague attempt to create one, I did not see the benefit of them because there was no evidence that boundaries would make any difference to my life.

And so, in comes the unraveling.

Boundaries was yet another distinctive knot related to motherhood. It is not the last knot we need to loosen because this knot is entwined with quite a few other broken threads—guilt; shame; vulnerability; a lack of understanding our values, ourselves, motherhood; control; and mental wellbeing.

Because it is related to so many other knots and encompasses our understanding of so much of what we have already discussed in *Unraveling Motherhood,* the question of boundaries is left to the end of this book. So, what are boundaries and why do we need them?

Unravel

To understand if we need boundaries in our life, we can ask ourselves a few questions to figure out if we have any already in place. Answering yes to any of these questions may mean that you will benefit from placing boundaries in your life.

Yes ☐ No ☐   Do you feel overwhelmed, stressed, heading towards burnout?

Yes ☐ No ☐   Do you feel as if your child, partner, or others run your life?

Yes ☐ No ☐   Do you feel as though your life is not your own?

Yes ☐ No ☐   Do you feel taken advantage of by those you love?

Yes ☐ No ☐   Do you resent others for being so demanding and insensitive to your needs?

Yes ☐ No ☐   Do others' needs seem much more urgent than yours?

Yes ☐ No ☐   Do you tend to meet others' needs before your own?

Yes ☐ No ☐   Do you question the importance of your own needs?

Yes ☐ No ☐   Do you try to avoid disappointing others?

Yes ☐ No ☐   Do you aim to avoid confrontation?

Yes ☐ No ☐   Do you believe your feelings are not valid compared to the feelings of others?

Yes ☐ No ☐   Do you get upset if someone dislikes you or is critical of you?

Yes ☐ No ☐   If someone criticizes you, do you believe that their criticism is true?

Yes ☐ No ☐   Do you let other people define you?

Drawing A Line

A boundary is something that will separate me from you, you from me, and us from the exhaustion of motherhood. Our physical space, our emotions, our needs, and our responsibilities, all become encroached on as we move deeper and deeper into motherhood. They need definite boundaries so that we can take care of ourselves and honor our own needs.

Like drawing a line, boundaries set our limits and protect us from being overloaded, resentful, or depleted.[1] We can, and should, create this space for ourselves so that we can make our own decisions, sit with our own feelings, and give ourselves what we need physically, spiritually, and emotionally. It does not always feel good to set these limits, especially at the beginning when we first put a boundary in place, and we haven't seen the benefit yet, but highlighting our limitations will help preserve our emotional and physical energy. Without drawing the line, we may become so overwhelmed that we lean closer towards avoidance rather than boundaries. Avoiding people, events, and problems, is a short-term measure which only prolongs unnecessary anxiety and stretches out our overwhelm. It is not a solution.

We have yet to have that necessary conversation here about valid and genuine self-care (which we will), but it's vital to know that healthy boundaries are a form of honest self-care as we prioritize our needs, allowing ourselves to navigate and release the worry or stress of saying no. Not only that, but boundaries create realistic expectations of what our friends, family, even our kids, can ask of us. Boundaries create safety and security as we give ourselves permission to remain within our self-care zone of manageable and comfortable opportunities.

Boundaries are not ultimatums we give to our friends and family, or to ourselves. They are not power struggles but are there to empower us to live in a way that is true and honest to our values in life. Where in our lives do we need boundaries?

Physical Boundaries

When we first think of boundaries, many of us have an idea of what the physical side of that looks like. It includes our personal space, our homes, our physical needs, and our comfort with touch. Kids have a unique ability to overstep the mark when it comes to our physical boundaries, but they have to learn about their own needs before they can even consider anyone else's, so it is only natural that they will want to stay as close to us for as long as possible. In many ways, our connection with them is their ultimate comfort. As their primary carer, we are the person that they come to for nurture and interaction. Both of which we may have a limited supply of throughout the day and we might yearn for space away from the unnecessary touching, sensory overwhelm, and constantly being needed.

The lack of physical personal space in those first few years of motherhood was quite the unexpected experience. I wondered if I spent my toddler years crawling around the legs of my mother like a lost cat and she assures me that I did. However, knowing this is something we all experience does not particularly help us with the child at our ankles. Instead of encouraging my kids to recognize I needed this boundary, I would quickly add an excuse, "I have hot coffee" or "The stove is on" or "I'm working," anything to assuage the guilt of saying no and protecting my needs. It took a long time for me to feel ok with saying, "Not now. I need some space." Understanding that we need to validate these boundaries is a knot so tight that it can be difficult to unravel. When we consider how a healthy physical boundary might appear, we can think of saying something like:

- "I am really tired right now. I need a minute to sit down on my own."

- "I need to eat. Please give me ten minutes to have a sandwich."

- "Can you please not sit on my lap right now. I need a bit of space."
- "Please don't go into my bedroom without asking me."

Emotional Boundaries

Emotional boundaries are a little more complicated because they deal with that hidden and unlimited ability as a mother to soak up everyone else's problems, emotions, and drama. Our emotional boundaries come down to understanding and recognizing how much emotional energy we have to help others combat those sticky situations in their lives. We need to learn how to accept our limitations in validating the feelings and experiences of others. When we respect our own emotional boundaries, there is give and take in our relationships. It is both sharing and supporting and can look something like:

- "Today's been hard. I really need you right now. Can we talk?"
- "I am sharing my feelings with you, and you are shutting me down. I don't feel respected."
- "I don't have the mental or emotional capacity to talk about this right now."
- "I understand you are having a tough time, but I can't focus right now. Can we talk about this later?"

Time Boundaries

Time is a boundary so many of us struggle with, especially in motherhood, when our time is linked so intrinsically with that of our kids. From playdates, birthday parties, and extracurricular activities, our time is spread over more than one life. We support our partner with their job and their commitments while also balancing our own commitments with our own careers. Where do we find the time for ourselves?

After years of neglecting my limitations, my time boundary was a quickly untangled knot when it came to my self-care. When Devin was one and a half, I was at my most exhausted and most overwhelmed. I was knee deep in twisted mental health and took absolutely zero care of my own needs. So much so that I ended up ignoring symptoms of a chest infection and found myself in hospital with double pneumonia. It was the hardest life lesson I have ever learned.

It took lying in a hospital bed with a hacking cough, being woken at 5am for medications and realizing I could barely breathe after sucking the life out of oxygen tank after oxygen tank, for me to recognize the importance of protecting my time and allocating a decent proportion to my own needs. Our time may very well be our most valued commodity.

Setting time boundaries means prioritizing and not overcommitting your precious time and understanding exactly how much of your day you are willing to give to other areas of your life. These boundaries can look like:

- "No, Allegra can't come for a playdate on Friday."
- "I would love to help, but I'm not available then. Can we arrange it for another time?"
- "I can only stay for half an hour."
- "I can't make it. Saturday is our family time."

Relationships Boundaries

When it comes to our relationships, we can define what we are comfortable with in regard to our emotional, physical, and intellectual boundaries. Setting boundaries with our partner, our friends, and our family members is a healthy thing to do, despite it sometimes feeling objection-able. We need to remember that healthy limits in all our relationships positively affects our confidence and self-esteem while nurturing us with safety, trust, compromise, cooperation, and support. These boundaries are likely to work both ways as we respect each other's needs and create a healthy dynamic.

If we find ourselves being consistently pulled into drama, arguments, or debating with friends or family, we may need to set boundaries. The same concept applies if we feel we are being taken advantage of or constantly fixing other peoples' problems. There should be a balance in our relationships, the necessary give and take, and most importantly, understanding.

Intellectual Boundaries

Our intellectual boundaries are not something we often give much consideration to because it is difficult to recognize when they are being violated. It comes down to others' respecting our boundaries when it comes to our thoughts, ideas, and even our curiosity. When we are crit-icized, belittled, or dismissed in our thoughts, our boundaries are being broken. Maintaining our intellectual boundaries can look like:

- "You're not listening to me."
- "You're twisting my words. That's not what I meant."
- "This is not the right time or place to talk about this."
- "We can disagree. I respect that we have different opinions."

When The Line is Broken

Now that we know where our boundaries lie, how can we figure out if we have poor boundaries? Not recognizing our limits reminds me of growing up in the eighties when the front door was always open and we would run in and out through the house, out to the back garden, up the stairs, back to the kitchen to raid the fridge, and then back out to the front to play on the grass across from our house. It was a whirlwind of constant motion, with my mum shouting after us to stop running through the house, and either stay in or out, but most of all, to close the damn door! We were continuously attacking my mum's boundaries. The door was wide open, and we were pouring in and out not thinking or caring about what my mum needed in that present moment. And why would we? We were kids. Boundaries, rules, and consideration were at the bottom of our list when we needed a tennis racket to play rounders, or a scarf to mark our base to play cops and robbers.

But it is not up to everyone and everything around us to close that door. That comes down to us, and us alone. We have to learn or regain control of that closed door because we are the only one with the key to keep it shut or narrowly open it if we so wish. Having control over that front door and keeping it closed means, we are protecting our boundaries and navigating our limits in a way that is right for us. If we don't tell them, how will others know what we need from them in order to protect our boundaries?

So, when we were happily playing outside, my mum would shut the door.

The Misunderstandings of Boundaries

The funny thing about drawing that line to make sure that someone doesn't cross it in a way that would negatively impact on our space, time, or emotions, is that we are often afraid to tell someone they are crossing that line. We are held back by that idea that we have to take every piece of well-intentioned but unsolicited advice when it comes to our parenting with a pinch of salt. Grin and bear it, but why should we allow someone to effectively breach our boundaries with advice that is unlikely to help and will leave us shamed, stigmatized, hurt, anxious, or worried?

I had extremely poor boundaries when I first became a mother. Spurred on by so many other knots of my unraveling, I kept quiet when I felt judged; I always said "yes" despite my anxious mind being unable to cope with all of the responsibilities landed on my shoulders; I was incapable of making decisions, and yet resented my actions and that of others when I did; and I felt a surging guilt because I felt the world looked at me as a bad, poor, ineffectual mother.

Some of my boundaries were either led by fear and rigidity, meaning the door was firmly locked with a brick wall built alongside it as I attempted to protect myself. However, these walls kept out those I should have trusted to help me, no matter how often they rang the bell. On the other hand, different boundaries were porous, and that door swung open like the door of my 1980's childhood. Everything ran through that door and knocked me over as I took on the shame, the guilt, the callous remarks, the toxic friendships, the fear, and the disrespect.

Despite it being so very obvious to me now, I did not know why I needed boundaries, and I did not know how to close that door. I had it in my head that I had to let everyone in. Don't we need a village when a baby is born? Shouldn't we always ask for help? Well, the village was there, so the door was wide open. Except, and this is the thing about boundaries, not everyone or everything is good for us, especially in early motherhood. Our boundaries are needed so that we can communicate our wants and needs to reflect this huge life change.

Unraveling our limits comes with a few misunderstandings which we have to unknot before we can start closing that door and putting our boundaries in place.

Boundaries are not selfish. While, it can feel selfish, it is not an egotistical act to focus on our own limits, and request they be respected by others.

Boundaries are not a punishment. We don't use boundaries to punish those around us for taking advantage of us or overstepping the mark. Boundaries are a proactive way to protect our values, goals, needs, and wants.

Boundaries are not controlling. Boundaries are not a way for us to exert control over another person and dictate what they can and cannot do. It is about creating and choosing healthy behaviors over our own actions, and not the actions of others.

Our boundaries make us strong and connect us to ourselves and what we truly need to care for ourselves, to build on our confidence, self-esteem, and self-worth.

Unravel

How do you know when your front door is wide open?

- You say "yes" when you really want to say "no."

- You agree with someone when you really want to disagree.

- You give away too much of your time, energy, and physical and emotional space.

- You feel guilty, taken for granted, and make bigger sacrifices than others.

- You feel overly responsible for the actions and emotions of others.

- You are fearful of what others think of you.

- You overshare or have trouble making decisions.

- You are exhausted but don't take time to rest.

- You satisfy the needs and expectations of others without looking at what you need.

- There are one too many toxic relationships in your life.

Boundaries in Motherhood

Boundaries are significant whether we are parents or not and they play out in so many different areas of our lives. With our family, our partners, work colleagues, friends, and acquaintances. However, there is an added shift in our boundaries as we add significant groups to our daily lives who can unknowingly drift through a broken boundary line. It's the parents at the school gate, teachers, the school bus driver, right down to the neighbor you only see as you pass by on the school run, all of whom become added elements in unknotting our boundaries and making sure they are well and truly secure.

Let's also remember that we need to refine and set boundaries with our kids, who also need to learn how to set their own boundaries. By having healthy boundaries ourselves, we teach our children to tune in to their own needs and establish personal boundaries as they get older.

My kids, as yet, have little to no understanding of boundaries when it comes to their parents. We are at their beck and call, and they do not yet feel as though it is inappropriate to pay us a visit while on the loo, and question, albeit politely, why we are not playing with them after we have spent a grueling ten hours at work. They do not yet understand why we would not want 325 close contact hugs in the space of five minutes, and they have yet to comprehend why there are family and household "rules," and why sometimes we would like five minutes to have an adult conversation together.

Having poor boundaries not only affect us, but also our children. Dr. Lisa Coyne is a clinical psychologist who has worked with families for 20 years and is also a mother. Her expertise in unraveling boundaries is much appreciated, especially in relation to the knots which are not always implicitly implied or understood when it comes to boundaries and the effect they have on our mental wellbeing.

"Poor boundaries, behaviorally, can contribute to child behavioral problems," Lisa tells me. "They can be associated with permissive parenting and poor emotional boundaries, for example, an unwillingness to experience negative emotion in ourselves or in our child, can lead to parental accommodation, and intrusive or overcontrolled parenting in families. These situations can result in raising anxious children.

"Also trying to parent 'perfectly' can lead to burnout, which is a hot topic these days. As is, helicopter parents or snowplow parents who don't allow independence and growth or who don't provide opportunities for children to learn skills by facing adversity.

"It can be hard to parent based on societal 'rules' about what parenting should look like, because that might be associated with lots of social comparison and self-evaluation, rather than sensitive and responsive parenting based on what your child, and your family, might need."

Understanding our boundaries whether it is with our kids, our parents, or the members of the PTA, come from within us first and foremost. No one will know our boundaries unless we communicate them.

Unraveling Limitations

The interesting quirk about boundaries is that we already have them. They are in our minds, and partially activated. We need to create a habit of understanding and establishing a routine with our boundaries, telling everyone what they are. But before we get stuck into actively working with our boundaries, there are a few things potentially holding us back from recognizing our limits, putting a cap on them, and feeling good about setting these boundaries. Most notably, these knots are fear and guilt.

Because of the misconception that it is unfair, harsh, and sometimes cruel to build boundaries, we feel we may be pushing people away or negatively impacting on our relationships. We think that we are letting people down, not being the productive women that we are "supposed to be," not meeting societies standards, not "good enough," or not deserving of the time we spend valuing ourselves. In fact, the opposite is true. Healthy boundaries in life means we are not jeopardizing our values and are shown the trust and respect we need to maintain our wellbeing.

And yet, because of the way in which society spurs on motherhood with a narrative subjectively met with the idea that we are "indulging" or "splurging" when we take care of ourselves, we are in effect told that we are not worthy or deserving of self-care which includes advocating for those boundaries. It is no wonder that we are bombarded with unwanted thoughts and emotions which can take up a disproportionate amount of our time as we allow these thoughts to spiral. They drain our energy leading us to avoid doing something which may be painful or uncomfortable in the interim but with a long-term gain.

Short Term Discomfort vs Long Term Gain

Setting boundaries begins with a conversation. Depending on the boundary, the conversation can be loaded with overthinking. What will I say? How will they react? Why is this so stressful? It's daunting setting boundaries, I know. Over the years, I have had uncomfortable conversations and have not been able to find the right words to express myself well enough to counter a retaliation of criticism, disapproval, or plain and simple hurt.

I have learnt that I do not manage these conversations well during a face-to-face encounter but have fared better with a series of texts and a few emails. Barry has been the recipient of many of these texts, and in many ways, as we set boundaries with each other, it was a good learning experience knowing we had full trust in each other already to navigate these conversations loaded with emojis. Of course, there was discomfort, but it was more manageable in a way because we each had the stage to talk without being interrupted or overthinking.

There have also been times when I dropped the issue of expressing the validity of the boundaries I needed because I was not being understood and the flood of emotions that came with the misunderstanding led to uncertainty and subsequently to me shutting the matter down. No boundaries were set as a result.

This short-term discomfort becomes balanced when the benefits of setting boundaries become visible. The long-term benefits of knowing and validating your limits boosts your mood, your self-esteem, your wellbeing, adds value to your goals, builds your respect for yourself, your compassion, and creates a finer balance in life with less stress, worry, exhaustion, and burnout.

The long-term benefits are exactly what we need in life, and if we are to avoid those potential awkward and uncomfortable moments, we are not helping ourselves to untangle this great big knot which, when released, can stitch up an entirely new pattern of selfcare.

The Boundary of Guilt and Shame

Even though we know it may only be temporarily uncomfortable, and that setting boundaries is good for our wellbeing, we can still be hit with those feelings of guilt or shame when attempting to close that door. It is like holding the door open for someone in the supermarket only for another ten people to walk through as you keep the door ajar. We continue to hold the door because it is polite, we would feel guilty if we let go and walked away. In the same way, we hold our own door open and allow the unwanted thoughts and emotions of guilt and shame to walk through too.

Thankfully, we can take stock of these feelings and explore why they are triggers and blocks for us in setting boundaries which will no doubt support us in life. First of all, what are guilty thoughts and shameful thoughts?

- Guilty thoughts can sound something like: *I did a terrible thing. I shouldn't have done that. I regret what I did.*

- Shameful thoughts can sound like: *I'm a bad person. I don't deserve their love, support, or forgiveness. I am unworthy.*

When we notice guilt leading our negative thoughts such as feeling sad, lonely, and apologetic, we can begin to overcompensate in an effort to make amends. When we feel ashamed, we move into a spiral of anxiety, hopelessness, and hating ourselves. We isolate ourselves away from others and avoid anything that will irritate those feelings. Both guilt and shame block us from setting healthy boundaries. With guilt, we could lean towards opening that door and holding it open. With shame, we lock that door right up and refuse entry to everyone and everything, creating one big barrier of the unhealthy variety.

Ask yourself:

- What have you learned about guilt and shame from your past, your friends and family, and from society as a whole?
- Where have you noticed guilt or shame in your life?
- How do you ordinarily respond to guilt or shame?
- What are the long-term costs or challenges associated with your response to guilt or shame?

Unraveling these feelings is about noticing ourselves and our reactions and feelings to situations. "This isn't about changing thoughts," says Lisa, "that would be counterproductive. It's more about changing our relationship to our thoughts, and about focusing on the big picture such as on our parenting values, and letting those values, instead of moment-to-moment interactions, guide our behavior over time."

In this manner, we are going to notice when these feelings come up for us and how we respond to them.

- What thoughts show up when you recognize guilt or shame within yourself? For example, *"I wish I didn't do that."*

- What emotions show up when you recognize guilt or shame within yourself? For example, *sadness or remorse.*

- How do you ordinarily react when you recognize guilt or shame? For example, *do you overcompensate in helping someone?*

- How does this response impact you? For example, *do you go into overdrive and work harder?*

- How can you respond compassionately when you recognize guilt or remorse? For example, *by recognizing and accepting why you feel guilty while moving towards your motivation.*

The idea here is to recognize the blocks we have in setting our necessary boundaries, accepting that we are worthy of being prioritized, and overcoming any uncertainty we have concerning those facts. We may believe that we do not deserve to set boundaries, that we will become overly self-involved by prioritizing our needs, or that we are simply too busy and have no time to identify what boundaries we need, or even that boundaries will block us from being that productive, empowering mother that we need to be.

We not only deserve, but also need boundaries in motherhood. They are a necessity, not just for us, but for our whole family. A woman who mothers on her own terms with positive and supportive wellbeing, is quite frankly, an asset to any household. Mothering on our own terms does not mean that we are too self-involved to consider others. We will not become insensitive to the needs of others but will acknowledge, support, and honor the boundaries of those around us. And yes, we are all damn busy, but being productive, diligent, or balancing a hectic home, is not empowerment.

Boundaries are empowering and we need to consistently remind ourselves of that.

Unravel

When we are stuck in an uncertainty spiral which can block us from creating the necessary boundaries in life, we can take small steps to sit with those feelings of discomfort and tolerate the uncertainty to move on.

When thinking about boundaries, or situations in life that make you uncomfortable, overextended, or exhausted, what question arose in your mind about this uncertainty?

_____

_____

_____

What feelings, beliefs, or thoughts did you feel or experience?

_____

_____

_____

What sensations did you feel in your body?

_____

_____

_____

What advantages or problems did you experience?

_____

_____

_____

Defining Boundaries

There is no single way to unravel boundaries. We all have different elements in our lives which warrant varying degrees of boundaries, at various times in our lives, and at multiple levels. It is in trying to figure out where we need boundaries that we learn quite a bit about ourselves such as our values, beliefs, how much we care about certain issues, how much we respect and prioritize our relationships, and how far we will go to nurture these boundaries.

Defining our boundaries is an emotional connection. We are often triggered into creating boundaries. I have a distinct aversion to anything being put directly in my face, so when my kid's thrust books, papers, Lego blocks, or even their hands within an inch of face, I tell them I do not like that behavior from anyone, and if they continue to do it, I will be upset and leave the room. They now stop when I ask them not to do it as they have slowly recognized that this is a boundary with a consequence. A rule with an expectation set to avoid feeling triggered, overwhelmed, or overloaded when my personal space is breached. Not all boundaries are simple and straightforward examples such as this, and it is the bigger issues that we can have trouble defining and navigating.

Unravel

We don't sit down with a pen and paper and write down a list of where we want to build up boundaries with friends and family. Boundaries occur as a result of something that we recognize through our reaction to a behavior, either ours or someone else's. If we feel awkward at an event and wish we had said no to the invitation, we need to look closer at why we feel uncomfortable and why we did not say no in the first place. We need to look at our boundaries when it comes to socialization, or our willingness to be available.

Defining our boundaries can fall under varying ideas:

- Routines, habits, and limits that protect us from becoming triggered.

- Beliefs and values about what we are comfortable with.

- Our likes, dislikes, and preferences that are unchanging.

- Moments in time when we have hit a "wall" and start conducting ourselves in ways that are out of character.

- Closed doors and limits that contribute to feelings of safety and well-being.

- Self-boundaries to manage and monitor our behavior, choices, and interests.

Setting Boundaries

Setting boundaries is a commitment to yourself, so I encourage you to identify where you need boundaries and have the strength, courage, and tenacity to set boundaries in place. Again, the short-term discomfort of doing this will be outweighed by the long-term benefits to your wellbeing. Now that we have learned to recognize when and where we need boundaries, how exactly do we set them? Let's unravel this together with an example of a mum friend who oversteps the mark with her observations on motherhood.

1: Identify an issue.

Setting healthy boundaries can really only be done when we identify an issue in need of a closed door. Unless we have grown up with good role models who have shown us how to create and hold boundaries, we may only realize that our limits are challenged when the line has been crossed.

Let's say we feel overburdened by how a friend speaks to us about the way we parent. In the beginning, we may feel as though they are being supportive and offering advice in the way mum friends are supposed to. Before long, we notice their tone of voice is sharp, their words are grating and corrective, their behavior is judgmental and arbitrary.

2: Figure out how this issue is affecting you.

We set boundaries to protect ourselves from influences which can negatively impact our lives. With boundaries we are asking to be respected, trusted, and treated well. They are the rules that show what we will and will not tolerate. They are not rules we impose on others but a level to which we adhere to personally.

We can learn to spot when toxic friendships in motherhood can have a way of manipulating and hijacking our lives without us even knowing it. When friendships move in a negative direction, our self-worth is challenged, our beliefs are questioned, and we may feel worthless, leaving us feeling shamed for how we parent.

3: Name what you don't like about this issue.

We help our younger kids to understand their emotions by encouraging them to put names to their feelings. When setting boundaries, we need to help ourselves to name those feelings too. We may recognize that a limit has been hit, but not understand why we are not comfortable with this. By naming what we do not like about an issue and the associated feelings that are conjured up, we advocate for building a boundary in that area of our lives.

So, with our toxic friend, we may not appreciate their poor advice, or their glaring attitude towards either how we parent, or what our kids do. Those side-eyes, glares, and judgmental comments such as "My daughter would never do that," only make us feel bad, worthless, flawed, when we know that is not the case.

4: Understand your area of responsibility.

When we talk about our area of responsibility, we are referring to the areas of our life we have control over, which is primarily us—our actions and our emotions. It helps to remember that we have no control over what other people think, feel, or do. With our toxic friend, we cannot control their behavior, but we can highlight what we are accepting of, and bullying and toxicity are not on that list.

Setting boundaries is not about controlling the behavior of another person but creating boundaries that allow us to be ourselves.

5: Highlight what you would prefer to happen.

Now that we have figured out the issue and why it is affecting us, we can think about what we would prefer to happen. Ideally, in this scenario, we would want the belittling conversations to end. Our options are to encourage a sway of conversation such as taking the topic of motherhood off the table when you meet with this person.

If keeping the friendship is important to you, then this is a boundary you will need to investigate with them. Otherwise, we are looking at breaking contact with a friend who is acting in a toxic manner. Sometimes, breaking up with friends is a boundary that we need.

6: What are the consequences?

We can decide what will happen if someone breaks our rules (which they are likely to do, especially if we have left others to guess our boundaries. No one is a mind reader). This decision is a little complex because for the boundary to work, we need to be proactive in following through on the consequences. If this friend continues to make you feel bad about your parenting, a consequence could be ditching the friendship altogether. If that is too harsh of a consequence, you could have a direct conversation about your feelings when certain things are said and include the consequence that will be enforced if your boundary is not met.

7: Set a boundary.

"If we keep having conversations like this, I can't be your friend anymore." This is not a conversation that will be smooth sailing, but this is how we set boundaries. The short-term discomfort for the long-term gain. When communicating our boundaries, include what the issue is, how we feel about it, what we would prefer to happen, and what the consequence will be if a boundary is crossed. If a friendship is worth saving, both you and your friend will recognize the importance of these boundaries (and they may have a few of their own).

8: Follow through.

Finally, a boundary needs maintenance. Oil the hinges on the doors, and ensure you follow through with a boundary and its consequence if necessary. You may need to reiterate your feelings, concerns, and boundaries with the party involved (and to yourself). There may be new rules for you to both follow. Maintaining boundaries means consistently respecting yourself to understand your boundaries are there for a reason.

9: Holding Boundaries.

Holding our boundaries is our responsibility and no one else's. We cannot expect anyone else in our household to respect or consider our boundaries especially if they are not aware of what they are. Upholding our boundaries can be the most complex part of this unraveling because it takes commitment and consistency.

While we hold the door closed, there are plenty of people who will push that door and try to open it. We may become so exhausted from the effort that we stop holding the door and allow them back in. It is a trial-and-error scenario in finding the right balance with our boundaries and the consequences. A test of strength and determination to reinforce our limits.

We may find that we need to reconsider the consequences or recommunicate our boundaries and realize that this is not always going to be an easy transition. It may become difficult, so it is important to remember why you set the boundary in the first place. Remind yourself of what you wished to gain from this boundary, and how it would affect your wellbeing.

The Closed Door of Motherhood

I never saw the benefit of my mum closing the front door when I was eight, apart from not letting the heat out. I would only open the door again and forget to close it anyway, but having that door closed was more than battling the annoyance of her kids and the whole neighborhood traipsing through her house. It was not a power struggle but a necessity and a boundary that we broke repeatedly.

I have learned a lot from my mum as I look back at how she mothered us and herself. When we would come home from school to the smell of cupcakes cooling on wire racks, I felt a hint of sadness because I loved to bake when I was a kid. I especially loved to bake with my mum but there the spongy cakes sat, baked with love without me. Unknown to me, my mum held the door open for me and my brother to share in the sticky joy of icing the pre-baked buns with her before dinner. Her boundary came in the gentle form of baking without us, meaning she had control over the chaos of the kitchen without young kids in tow, but she gave us the time and attention when letting us get our sticky hands into the icing bowl and lick the beaters.

She would tell us she was going upstairs to rest for a while, ask us to keep the noise and TV down, and she would close the door of her bedroom, creating the space and boundary she needed. She would tell us "No" when we begged to go to a friends' house at the absolute worst time. She created boundaries in a way that were a matter of family life and simply became the way it was for us and for her. She decided what way her motherhood would go, but I know from our countless chats on this transition that she unraveled, stitched up, and unraveled again, as we all do.

As I unravel myself, I look to her to see how she stitched up certain aspects of motherhood, balancing her boundaries along with her values, beliefs, triggers, and accepting her flaws and imperfections while confirming her knowledge that she was and is good enough. These have all been lessons for me to learn as I mother myself. An unraveling that I consistently go back to is the importance of recognizing that closed door of motherhood which encourages us not to feel as though we are abandoning, neglecting, or forgetting the needs of our children or our partner.

Over time, my mother's needs changed, and as our family dynamic altered alongside her, she naturally rebuilt the boundaries she needed. I can feel my own needs shifting as the girls grow older and our own dynamic changes. I can feel, as my experience of motherhood grows, as my needs shift, my wellbeing balances, and I become more flexible in my thinking, my boundaries are a guide, a protector, and a comforter developed through the knowledge that I am leaning so wonderfully towards living the life I want to live, being the mother I want to be, and accepting the woman in the mirror.

The door of motherhood does not always have to be closed, but you should be the only one in control of that lock. You can close the door on being taken advantage of, having to fix other people's problems, getting sucked into pointless and derivative arguments and heated debates, being overly concerned by other people's actions, or being a part of all the drama. You can, and will, do you!

chapter 7

Stitching Up

● Stitching Up

**To do the final things that are needed to complete
(something) in a successful way**

Dictionary, **Merriam-Webster**

T HERE IS, BY NO means, anything final about stitching up, no matter what the dictionary says. How many times have you stitched the
school crest on the kid's jumper only to find that it peels away after a few
washes? How many times have you pricked your finger on the needle?
How many times has a hem come loose? We are those loose stitches, life
is the gentle stabs on our finger, and we may find ourselves unraveling all
over again at other times in our life. Grief, turmoil, upheaval, the empty
nest, and unexpected change, all have a way of pulling on a frayed thread,
creating, or loosening knots. Our unraveling and stitching up is never
really done in the true sense of the word.

Accepting that this is not the end is quite an important part of this
entire transformation into and through motherhood. It is, and always
will be, a state of flux which we will change and grow with, over and
over again. It is my hope that we have unraveled useful thought patterns

throughout this book to help you approach these changing designs of life in a way that you will trust yourself, your voice, and your path in life.

All along, I have asked you to answer questions, to consider your thoughts, and to place you in front of yourself to find what you need in this life as mum. This is overwhelming, I know. I have been there as I jumped from knot to knot thinking I could unravel it all at once and be the centered, crafty, and enduring mother I aimed to be. It is not as simple as that. If that was the case, none of us would have any knots to unravel. Building ourselves, growing, learning, and being honest with ourselves is a long process, so don't expect to feel a weight lift immediately.

Added to that, we have thrown around some pretty big ideas here.

There are limits to how easily we can unknot these ideas, and knowing our limits is essential in all of this questioning and mindful consideration. We can do anything we set our mind to, but we cannot do everything. This entire unraveling is exhausting. Bear in mind, we have questioned life so internally and twisted and turned ideas which have left us feeling confused and overwhelmed. An unraveling in itself can become somewhat of a burden when we commit to it without setting a limit on how much we can mentally and emotionally consume. So, take your time with it. Approach it in a way that is comfortable and beneficial to you because what would be the point in tying up more knots than you are untangling.

Of course, there may have been more questions than answers throughout these pages. However, that is not necessarily a bad thing. The more questions we ask, the more we get to know ourselves, the more we unknot, the more we get to the root of our understanding. So, throughout these pages you may have felt:

My experience of motherhood is fine, I suppose. We're all healthy, we have a roof over our head. What do I really have to worry about, complain about, or question?

This was my initial response to therapy, to provoking my thoughts, and peeling back the layers of my past. My kids were healthy and happy. I was happily married. I had a good job. There was nothing explicitly wrong with my life. And yet, I was despondent, anxious, fearful, unfulfilled, and feeling inadequate. Why wasn't I grateful enough? What did I have to really complain about?

It is important to remember that all our experiences are valid, our feelings, our struggles, and our needs are valid. It is ok if you manage to get everyone out the door on time every day for the school run, and still feel out of control. We can manage our days and feel like life is good and still feel fearful or anxious. We can have wonderful days and still resent motherhood and all it has stolen from us. We can still have all kinds of big feelings and not know how to deal with them but still appear steady as a rock on the outside.

Stitching Up ⟶ It's ok to feel confused, have bad days, want more out of life. There is a freedom in being allowed to be honest and true not only with yourself but with those around you. Motherhood is messy. We are allowed to be messy too. It is in giving ourselves permission to show up cluttered, disheveled, and awkward that we may figure out how to unravel our knots.

My experience of motherhood is fine, I suppose. I have three kids. It's not like I haven't been here before with the overwhelm and complete exhaustion. I'm used to it.

Motherhood is not a burden as such, but it holds so much responsibility that we hide away how much we struggle with this change. Yes, we may become used to it but in the beginning, we are kicked into this entirely unknown territory and silently, almost valiantly, we keep how we experience motherhood a secret right through until the second, the third, the fourth is born. We smile, show up, and deliver, despite not wanting to, and we feel so terribly alone, unseen, and misunderstood. It is difficult to show our vulnerability and be seen in all of this overwhelm. We are hit with a pressure to be perfect accompanied by a fear of failure leading to chronic pain, anxious thoughts, self-sabotage, or worry. The responsibilities weigh heavy and the overwhelm becomes the burden.

Stitching Up ⟶ It is ok to ask for help, to let go a little, to recognize you are not alone. The belief that we will carry on regardless, is a false one. We do not have to pretend that we are fine.

My experience of motherhood is ok, I suppose. It is not what I expected, but what is?

The thing about expectation is that it is full of magical thinking. We expect life with kids to go one way and feel disappointment when it goes another. The problem is that our expectations of motherhood are so varied and filtered that the reality can be limited and filled with greying, blurred tones. We may end up with regret, dissatisfaction, disillusionment, and a whole host of other quandaries unless we figure out how we can influence our lives in a way that does not necessarily match our confused expectations, but rather meets a realistic outlook.

Stitching Up ⟶ It is ok to not know what our definition of success looks like, or to not know where we want to be in five years. It is ok to not have all the answers and to still feel lost. This progress is not straightforward. We will go backwards as much as we go forwards. There will be ups and downs, changes, and fluctuations along the way but every movement towards finding realistic expectations is a positive move.

My experience of motherhood is fine, I suppose. I don't know, I just can't think.

Having the mental capacity to show up every day is exhausting. We can so easily run out of that necessary head space to think about ourselves and rejuvenate those all-important mental and physical energy levels. How often do we forget about ourselves amid the laundry basket, the dinners, and replacing the toilet roll? All the while reciting an internal monologue of all the things to be done including greasing the squeaky hinge on the bedroom door. We can be in love with our children and mentally and physically exhausted at the same time.

Stitching Up ⟶ It is ok to get angry when someone tells you that you need self-care, a hot bath with a frothy coffee, a walk in the autumn leaves as you mindfully listen to the crunch beneath your feet. Beneath the well-intentioned thought, you cry thinking how can you find the time let alone the strength to do anything more than tumble into bed at 9pm. What we need is support and space. Time to be quiet, untouched, and to breathe.

In all, these thoughts are much more complicated and enlarged than the simple narrative beneath them. The point is that we may believe our issues are not as subjective, necessary, or worthy in comparison to others. The vital thing to remember is that your experience is valid and worthy of deeper introspective thought, unraveling, and delicate stitches.

Stitching up these thoughts and the barriers we have unearthed to create the life we envision for ourselves, does not come down to a few questions. It becomes entwined in actively reaching out for change in our lives.

Finally, let's look at stitching up motherhood by focusing on the most important element in all of this unraveling—you.

Following the Lack of a Pattern

There is no pattern. I feel as though I may have promised a bright and glossy, easy to follow pattern throughout this book. A pattern to structure your thoughts, ideas, and loose threads into a perfectly stitched design. There is no perfection in any of this unraveling. We will make mistakes, have bad days, experience strong emotions, fight with our partner, doubt ourselves, and change our minds. We may continue to struggle with understanding our identity, and not see ourselves so well in the mirror. We will need guidance and support from those around us, and all of that is perfectly ok because we are human.

So, there is no pattern, but there are plenty of skills we can learn to stitch up a pattern and let our curiosity clack our knitting needles together to create that inner calm, understanding, and forethought we are looking for. For the sake of the metaphor, I am going to call these skills "stitches."

When it comes to our lives, to our unraveling of motherhood, the pages are not written until you decide to write them. One day, one hour, one moment at a time. All I can do is help guide you with how to get those stitches on your needles.

Stitch 1 ⟶ Mothering Ourselves

In all of our motherhood, there is a child we cannot leave behind, and that is our own internal, lost child who has been crying to be nurtured since page one. Our inner child is shouting to be heard, seen, understood, and loved. Mothering ourselves is an opportunity to allow us to heal and make choices for our lives. It is showing up for yourself and taking that inner child by the hand.

Being our own mother centers around that love, encouragement, soothing, and healing of the vulnerable child within us. It is about allowing ourselves to feel rejection, humiliation, and hurt, while permitting ourselves to cry, get angry, and express ourselves in the utterly human ways we need to. It is responding to those core emotional needs of our bare, naked, and exposed selves.

In many ways, when we begin to engage with mothering and reparenting ourselves to give our inner self what it needs to feel safe, protected, and loved, we are at the beginning stages of writing our own pattern, or rewriting it, as the case may be.

Unknotting

Why do we need to mother ourselves? Understanding the value in mothering ourselves will encourage us to lean into this stitch:

- To understand and validate our experiences.
- To create new patterns of thinking to help us move forward.
- To heal wounds we may still be carrying.
- To encourage boundaries.
- To remove unhealthy patterns in our lives.
- To overcome negative self-talk.
- To make decisions without fear.

Simple Stitches to Mother Ourselves

Listen to Yourself

In all the noise of motherhood, we can struggle to listen to ourselves, meaning our needs are not met because we have not tuned in to what they are. Take the time to actively listen. All of parenting becomes "active" listening as we desperately try to hear one individual over the bedlam of parenting. It is exhausting when so many voices blur into one but failing to listen to ourselves means we may judge the feelings which come up for us without allowing ourselves to unravel them. Ignoring our inner child is one heavy knot. Make communicating with yourself a priority.

Believe in Yourself

Our self-doubt is such an overtightened knot in motherhood, mostly highlighted by the fact that we become so intrinsically responsible for the wellbeing of our children as well as our own. Self-doubt makes progress so much harder as it stops us from seizing the life we want. It stops us from making decisions, from picking up the phone to make that important call, to take that step towards the future we are internally excited by. Believing in ourselves is another one of those motivational quotes found on an early Sunday morning scroll that I have long detested as though we can simply throw our shoulders back and say yes to everything. Self-doubt is a barrier that can be a little high to jump.

Remember, self-doubt is there to protect us from the upset we fear. We can embrace our self-doubt and still believe in ourselves, knowing that we can and will make mistakes, but that we are showing up amid the challenges. Doubt is a thinking trap which we will unknot further along our stitching up. In the meantime, know that your doubts are not true and are led by fear-fueled stories we tell ourselves.

Create Space for You

Motherhood begins with the most protective and nurturing of spaces as our babies are born from the warmth of our womb. How sharp and sterile is it when we emerge from that safe space to the sensory overload of the world? In mothering ourselves, we can recreate this safe space for ourselves by giving us permission to let our guard down and be so viscerally raw as we expound the emotions that build up over time. We can give ourselves this opportunity within our minds and within a physical space in our home. Creating space for you means creating those boundaries to allow yourself to be. To simply be.

Honor Your Unraveling

The unraveling process is not easy. I will not deny that. In mothering yourself, you can honor your growth as you unravel. This growth will happen in your own space and in your own time and is not to be compared with anyone else's progress on their own transformative psychological change. Respect that it will take time to process this entire unraveling.

Keep Moving Forward

In life, we may have very few cheerleaders. If those on the side-lines of your life are not cheering for you loudly, do not be afraid to cheer for yourself. We will face so many challenges throughout motherhood that we need as much encouragement as possible to face our fears, overcome adversity, and the ups and downs of life, so that you stay on track and focus on the path you want to follow.

In the same manner, celebrate yourself with every small win. Every knot you unravel, that's a win, every dinnertime without a fight, that's a win, every step closer to your dream, that's a win. Celebrate all of the wins and remind yourself of how proud you are of yourself.

When we understand the importance of showing up for ourselves, we can see how our own internal mothering can reflect so heavily on how we parent our children. Loving ourselves encompasses kindness, listening, compassion, gentleness, unconditional love, understanding, independence, growth, and advocates for a healthy balance in our lives. All of which are particularly helpful as we guide and raise children.

Stitching Up

Simple methods to mother ourselves:

- Journaling, allowing yourself to write in a stream-of-consciousness manner without censoring your thoughts.

- Physically comfort yourself with a warm drink, a nourishing meal, and be mindful of your actions.

- Get fresh air and exercise daily.

- Take a break from social media, the news, and any outside influences that impact on your wellbeing in a negative way.

- Listen to relaxing, soothing, or uplifting music.

- Give yourself the necessary time and space to think, read, meditate, and be mindful.

- Activate your mind by doing puzzles, reading, or mindful coloring.

- Speak to yourself kindly and encourage yourself in all you do.

- Laugh at yourself and give yourself permission to play and be silly.

- Surround yourself with everything that gives you comfort and joy.

- Ignite your passions by taking a masterclass (online or offline).

- Keep an eye on your energy and rest when needed.

- Create a nest for those times you need to sit with a hot coffee and a blanket. Make it your "spot."

- Create a comforting and relaxing bedtime routine.

Stitch 2 ⟶ Self-Acceptance

With mothering ourselves I have found that acceptance is a prominent stitch in all of this unraveling. Not only do we live in a world that is uncontrollable and quite probably out of control, but we are struck with this intense transformation and perpetually transformative experience that again can feel unmanageable at times.

We quite literally step into the unknown and yet are expected to know it all. It becomes, quite quickly, an overwhelming experience with inexplicably, large emotions so knotted and stuck that it is no wonder that so many of us fall into a spiral of, "I hate this," "I can't do this," and "Why is this so damn hard?" We create barriers that prevent us from unraveling and build walls so concrete that our behaviors become misinterpreted or out of character. We are only trying to protect ourselves from the enormity of it all, but that only leads to exhausted despair.

The problem with suppressing or avoiding these big emotions is that the opposite in fact happens. We become so consumed by these thoughts and negative feelings that they expand and amplify and there is no escape from the world we are creating in our heads, which may not be the truth. For a long time, I believed I was pointless, that I was an afterthought to our family life, that my children and Barry did not need me. I believed if I walked into that field across from our home and kept on walking, they wouldn't miss me. It was simply not true, but I built up this idea in my head so much that it became all encompassing. I didn't allow myself space to unravel the emotions or the impulses which led my actions. It took a long time for me to recognize the importance of self-acceptance. Accepting myself for who I am and what I am capable of.

Unknotting

Acceptance plays a vital role in our mental wellbeing and unraveling of motherhood:

- Accepting the reality of our situation can help us unravel how to change it for the better, helping us to face challenges in a healthier manner.

- Acceptance does not mean we approve of a situation but accepting the situation can help us look for a solution.

- Acceptance encourages us to understand the situation rather than fight against it.

- Acceptance avoids inner conflict.

- Acceptance encourages us to be more self-aware.

- Acceptance means we begin to understand who we are, what our strengths and weaknesses are and become comfortable in our vulnerability.

- Acceptance reduces our self-criticism and increases our self-esteem and self-worth.

- Acceptance reduces the pressure and stress from perfectionism.

- Acceptance makes us happier.

Simple Stitches for Self-Acceptance

True self-acceptance means embracing who we are, without judgement, conditions, or exemptions. Acceptance is quite a tough knot of motherhood because we have been raised in that patriarchal world full of expectations and assumptions. Unraveling ourselves to the point of accepting our entire being, flaws and all, while the ideologies and myths of motherhood peer over us, is easier said than done. Acceptance was one giant knot for me, that when pulled, released the tension on my entire motherhood.

Acceptance takes an enormous amount of effort as we motivate ourselves to acknowledge something for what it is despite being uncomfortable, unhappy, or angry with the situation, thought, emotion, or with ourselves. At the stage of acceptance, we move to work effectively to maneuver the situation as best we can. With acceptance we lean closer to the necessary change and reduce the negative impact of the situation.

Avoid Judgement

We can distribute our experiences into the good or bad corner and offer up labels and judgements. To accept ourselves or our situation, we have to cut judgement out and see the situation for what it is. We can fall down a rabbit hole of blame in motherhood but shaming ourselves will benefit no one. Criticizing ourselves harshly will rarely lead to a positive outcome and is also seldom the truth.

Acknowledge Where You Are

We can think of acceptance as being passive, or giving up, but in reality, acceptance recognizes that life is a continual unraveling. We may be in the pits of sleepless nights with babies and toddlers who enjoy sporadic sleeping and blame ourselves for failing to sleep train our kids. In reality, we have little to no control over the sleeping habits of young children. Acknowledge where you are in your motherhood journey and the challenges you are and will face.

Recognize Your Capability

Without acceptance we sit with negativity, upset, and the inability to move forward. Positively shifting our mindset to appreciate our capabilities and the possibilities around us, we move away from harsh criticism.

Accept Is a Verb

Acceptance is about action, continual action. As our motherhood evolves, so does our recognition of ourselves and it never ends as we transform and mitigate throughout our years as a mother. Yes, it can be frustrating, difficult, and heart-breaking to repeatedly encourage ourselves to accept and let go of certain things, but like a muscle, the more we practice acceptance, the stronger we will get, and the easier it becomes. Remember, accept is a verb and by continually choosing to acknowledge our actions, emotions, thoughts, and situations, we are actively making space for us to navigate away from the resistance which can hold us back.

Stitching Up

Simple methods for self-acceptance include:

- **Acknowledge to transform.** When we speak aloud and validate our experiences and emotions, we take the power out of the situation.

- **Take stock.** After acknowledging, we move to questioning and understanding what we have control over.

- **Acceptance of what is.** Then, we commit to accepting our reality for what it is.

- **Tuned in.** Finally, we tune into our body and use our five senses to understand how this situation affects us.

Stitch 3 ⟶ Self-Compassion

With self-compassion we give to ourselves that which we would give to a good friend. The helping hand, the kind word, the shoulder to lean on, and a random packet of wipes out of the multipack. Giving to ourselves always seems a little harder. It is difficult enough to show up every single day and multiple times throughout the night to pop a fallen soother back in or rub the back of a child who had a nightmare. We compromise with ourselves and make impossible choices, but we are rarely consciously kind to ourselves.

Self-compassion can come in the form of:

- Choosing what is best for you.

- Understanding why anxious or worried thoughts appear for you.

- Recognizing what you need emotionally, physically, and spiritually.

- Knowing that it is ok to say "no" and to build boundaries.

- Believing in yourself and knowing you are capable of change.

- Recognizing that you will have hard days.

- Validating yourself—your experiences, emotions, and thoughts.

- Not having all of the answers.

- Making mistakes and learning from them.

- Resting.

Unknotting

Self-compassion seems like a no-brainer, so why do we have so many knots around being kind to ourselves?

Knot: Self-compassion wrongly appears indulgent, selfish, or an act of self-pity.

Knot: Self-compassion is about how we relate to ourselves and others. It can remind us of times when we, or others, were not compassionate to us.

Knot: Self-compassion can be wrongly considered a weakness.

Knot: Self-compassion can again be wrongly considered as being unmotivated.

Knot: Self-compassion appears narcissistic. It isn't.

Simple Stitches for Self-Compassion

Self-compassion encompasses three elements which we will unravel. The first is *self-kindness,* which you would imagine we are all on board with at this stage of the century, but while we may do our best to encourage and spread kindness to others, self-kindness is one hell of knot we leave tightly wound up, especially when it comes to the harsh criticism that we give ourselves.

The second knot of self-compassion is recognizing how wonderfully *imperfect* we are which I hope we have unraveled sufficiently enough to help you unknot self-compassion. And the third, is *mindfulness* which I credit with being one of the cornerstones of my own unraveling. Mindfulness is the non-biased awareness of our experiences and an entire uplifting and lightening of the expectations of motherhood. So, let's stitch this up a bit.

Self-Kindness

As simple as it sounds, self-kindness is showing kindness to ourselves when we struggle, fail, or our flaws are highlighted. In life and in motherhood, we will fall short of our own expectations regardless of the expectations that society adds on to us. Recognizing that judgment, critique, and negativity will not benefit us in any way, we can show ourselves patience, kindness, and warmth instead. We can be accepting of our limitations and acknowledge when we are having a difficult time by being compassionate towards ourselves.

Recognizing Our Humanity

Our human nature can be a blessing or a curse depending on whether we accept it. We are not alone in any aspect of our humanity since much of what we do is a shared experience. When we accept ourselves, warts, and all, in all our imperfection, we can see that we are not alone in being flawed, having big unrecognizable emotions, and battling fluctuating thoughts. Understanding our humanity as a method of self-compassion highlights that we are all struggling, inadequate, learning, and continuously moving forward.

Mindfulness

Mindfulness is often wrapped up with a bit of confusion as it gets lumped in with meditation, but its explicitly different in cause and effect. It encompasses identifying our thoughts as opposed to reacting to them. We need this mindful interaction of being aware of our thoughts and emotions to avoid rumination and catastrophizing. Mindfulness leads us to self-compassion as we positively balance our experiences and emotions. Through mindfulness, we can keep our feelings in check when upset occurs. We can open ourselves to curiosity and interest as we unravel our emotions, and with mindfulness, we are offered the opportunity to refocus our perspective.

Our compassionate self can be hindered by unwanted thoughts and emotions making it challenging to nurture ourselves. We can access and recognize our compassionate self by asking a few questions to help us notice when we are being compassionate towards ourselves. Like the self-acceptance muscle, the more we actively notice our compassionate self, the easier it is to engage with it.

- What thoughts show up for your compassionate self? For example, do you hear yourself say, "I understand why I feel this way," or "It's ok that this hurts right now."

- What emotions show up for your compassionate self? For example, do you feel calm, content, relief, supported, happy, positive?

- What are the go-to actions for your compassionate self? For example, do you give yourself space to rest, are you gentle with yourself, do you intentionally listen to yourself?

- What is the impact of engaging with these compassionate self-actions? For example, do you give yourself time for self-care?

- How can you nurture and engage with your compassionate self?

Stitching Up

Simple methods of self-compassion include:

- Take active care of yourself.
- Accept yourself as you are.
- Be fair to yourself.
- Accept that struggle is normal.
- Practice mindfulness.
- Refocus long term goals.
- Realize no one is perfect.
- Avoid self-criticism.
- Stand up for yourself.
- Put your inner critic to bed.
- Build strong connections.
- Embrace yourself.
- Love yourself.

Stitch 4 → Self-Care Zone

We all know the tired mother who spends weeks running around with an ever-ballooning list of things to do, stuff to buy, people to remember, on particular days, in a convenient order, on round two, before closing time, before pick-up, before it's sold out, and the extra, all the extra swirling and piling and falling. God forbid anything is forgotten.

We all know the tired mother who skipped another meal to beat the traffic, who counted more grey hairs, whose eyes are so tired they are sore and dry, who dusted and swept and decorated and baked and cleaned the entire house without a word, without a complaint, with an aching back and sore fingers.

The tired mother who kept the plates spinning in a seemingly effort-less way, the job, the job-job, the third job, the baby, the toddler, the preteen and the teenager, the partner, the grandparents, the neighbor, the friend, and not often enough, herself. Never enough herself.

But I have learnt, as I hope you have, that motherhood does not equal self-sacrifice. Yes, there are times, plenty of them, when our needs will be left to last but that does not mean we must remain sitting pretty at the end of the list forever. Our self-care matters because we matter. The message behind what self-care encompasses has gotten a little skewed over the years as we are sold an idea of self-care that has us reaching into our pockets. Self-care cannot be sold to us. Self-care is advocating for our needs and understanding that we need as much care as anyone else in our home. We need rest, grounding, headspace, physical space, time to unwind, and time to be silent and introspective.

In many ways, we can look at self-care as taking ownership over our own happiness, nurturing ourselves, and giving to ourselves what others may not. The unique element of self-care is that no one can tell you how to do it and its why I have been reluctant to add examples of self-care practices here. For some, self-care could be engaging in a curious debate about politics with an equally knowledgeable relative, for others it's playing an in-depth board game like *The Settlers of Catan* with friends, for me it can be making origami stars while listening to jazz.

It is safe to say, what will benefit one person emotionally and physically may not benefit another. The important thing to note is that self-care is as individual as you and if you are unsure of how to begin with a practice of self-care, I suggest you start small by listing the things you enjoy doing, the people you love to spend time with, the things you like to eat, the music you enjoy listening to, the activities you miss.

In this manner, you can find what lifts you, what will energize you mentally and physically. Self-care is restorative in nature. It is a necessity as it maintains a balance in our lives which can otherwise become heavily skewed in favor of burnout, stress, fatigue, overwhelm, and resentment.

It's the ultimate recharge and reset button.

Unknotting

We know the value in restorative self-care does not lie in bubble baths or frothy coffees. So, what areas of our lives do we need rest and nurture?

- **Physical rest.** Our body will tell us when it has had enough, but we need to know when our tank is empty before we are hit with exhaustion on the brink of collapse or burnout.
- **Mental rest.** Finding it hard to focus and brain fog are key signs we are struggling with mental fatigue. It is time to rest.
- **Emotional rest.** When we react rather than respond, it is a sure sign that we are emotionally drained.
- **Creative rest.** This is easily recognizable when we struggle to come up with new ideas or battle with direction.
- **Sensory rest.** The overwhelm of the external world can wreak havoc on our energy levels as sensory overload hits. Sensory rest often calls for disconnecting from sensory stimuli like noise, social media, too many voices.
- **Social rest.** When our energy is depleted or we are overly stimulated by the energy sensitives of others, we need to rest our social calendar and reconnect with ourselves.
- **Spiritual rest.** Likely to occur when we feel isolated, lonely, or disconnected.

Simple Stitches for Self-Care

Practicing self-care is about setting intention for ourselves to give to our minds and bodies what they need. We typically only tune in to actively pursuing self-care when we need it, but its best practiced before we get to that verge of it being a necessity. Little and often in line with self-compassion and we are pro-actively protecting ourselves from burnout.

Enjoy the Small Things

Self-care is about intentional action. That action does not need to be disproportionately expressive. I consider my afternoon coffee, after the homework is packed away and the kids are resting with the TV and a snack, as being part of my self-care. At this stage of the day, I am noticing that I am tuning in the rest I need after the bedlam of after school. The small things are equally, or more important than the grand gestures. Enjoy and celebrate the small occasions, accomplishments, and successes.

Be Intentional

Recognize what you are doing as self-care, as something intentional for you and you alone in that moment. Purposefully and mindfully relax, rest, play, soothe, and listen.

Breathe, Sleep, and Get Active

Regular exercise, fresh air, restorative sleep, all positively benefit and influence our physical bodies and our mindset.

Consider Therapy

Self-reflection and processing our thoughts with a professional is a specific and worthwhile form of self-care, although not often recognized as such. Remember, self-care is about noticing your needs and showing up to actively put yourself first.

Continue the Practice

Even when times are overbearing and situations are tough, continue to practice self-care. It is in these difficult times that we become emotionally depleted making self-care harder to commit to, but ultimately this will be when it is most needed.

I understand within motherhood there are substantial barriers to practicing self-care, many of which include:

- Lack of support from a partner.

- Financial insecurity.

- Deep-rooted mother guilt.

- Lack of safe and reliable childcare.

- Children with unique needs that require our presence.

- The nature of the mental load of motherhood blocking our ability to secure and enjoy self-care.

- Experiencing self-care as an added chore.

- No motivation to add another commitment to our lives.

- A lack of awareness of our needs.

While self-care can be tricky to get in tune with there are uncomplicated ways to begin embracing the practice. Begin by making that list of things that inspire, enlighten, entertain, and motivate you. The things that draw you in. It could be coffee with a best friend, a solo walk by a lake, or watching the sunset from your back garden. Edit your list to include things you can do which do not require much financing or relying on other people for childcare. Find activities that are accessible to you, and things which you feel will actively support you. Take out anything that appears daunting, time consuming, or unsustainable. Now you have ideas which you can actively engage in.

Stitching Up

Remember, self-care can also include:

- Checking in with your emotions.
- Creating boundaries.
- Saying "no."
- Creating space.
- Choosing you.
- Focusing on what you can control.
- Forgiving past mistakes.
- Challenging your thought patterns.
- Choosing rest.

Stitch 5 ⟶ Mind Traps

I have been lost in traps of my own making. My thoughts were not my friend for a long time and triggered some unhealthy behavior which I still unravel, stitch up, and unravel, as I grow in confidence and mother myself as well as my children. We have more than 6,000 thoughts a day. Even the thought of such a high number is incredibly overwhelming. Add to that the knowledge that not all of these thoughts are positive or encouraging. In fact, our minds are guided towards negative thinking to protect ourselves from threat.

Hardwired Towards the Negativity Bias

Throughout history, we have evolved in a way that we have become fearful and deeply conscious of the negative. It is our tendency to more readily recognize the smallest of negative instances and to dwell deeper on these occasions than anything positive.

Our conscious recognition of negativity is the reason we are incredibly judgmental of ourselves, why we struggle to be our own cheerleader, why we helicopter parent our children, and why we dwell on those passing and fleeting negative comments. It is why we give more weight to the criticisms we hear about ourselves rather than the compliments.

The negativity bias is a deep-seated and ingrained habit of human nature as our ancestors had no choice but to pay attention to the danger around them. A saber-tooth tiger is thankfully not a threat we have to contend with anymore, but that negativity bias still sits within us, and we continue to stay tuned in to anything which may hurt us physically or emotionally. It's one of the reasons we are often on our guard in certain situations, why we listen to our gut instinct when we believe there is danger around us, and why we can get very much caught up in our thinking.

It is because of this psychological aspect of our thinking that we:

- Remember our traumatic experiences in greater detail compared to our positive experiences.
- Dwell on dark thoughts.
- React rather than respond to negative situations.
- Notice negative aspects about people, places, events, situations, or things.
- Become overwhelmed by our negative thinking.
- Think negative thoughts more frequently than positive.

- Potentially negatively impact our relationships.

- Respond more strongly to these negative thoughts in comparison to positive thoughts.

- And make it more difficult to maintain an optimistic outlook.

In all, the negativity bias can have quite a powerful effect on the decisions we make, our behavior, and our relationships with our family, friends, and kids. We lean towards this bias in even the simplest of matters of our lives. It can render us incapable of unraveling thoughts and can knot us up significantly with perceived risks and threats we believe surround us.

Also known as cognitive distortion, these automatic thoughts and assumptions can lead to unbalanced or blinkered thinking which can very easily distort our interpretation of the emotions which are coming up for us. We may misjudge why we feel angry, sad, guilty, anxious, or stressed. We may find ourselves, minute by minute managing our day with three kids. Getting them up, dressed, washed, fed, school lunches made, kitchen tidied, school bags ready, coats, shoes, hats, and out the door with a full face of makeup, only for one kid to effortlessly glance at the clock and say, "we're late" as you load them all into the car. Those two words will negate the huge effort and management we had over the morning, and we focus on being late to drop off by one minute. One measly minute can make our heads spiral into negative thinking. Overlooking the positives of the morning, we focus on one small minute. A thought, a thinking trap, which is likely to offset our day.

Luckily, we can find a way to unknot our thinking traps. We can learn to spot them and unravel these thought processes which are effectively badly stitched patterns of our thoughts.

Unknotting

Common types of thinking traps include:

All or Nothing Thinking. We can so easily split our thinking into it being one thing or another, but not accept that it may very well sit somewhere in the middle. Parenting does not sit within black and white thinking but rather in the various shades of grey. We may say to ourselves, "I'm such a bad mother," when we fail to recognize how absolutely amazing we actually are. This type of thinking is situational and, if something doesn't go to plan, it is automatically deemed a failure.

  Unknot: Instead of "I'm such a bad mother," say "No one is perfect."

Mind Reading. No one is a mind reader, but we can land ourselves in a trap by jumping to conclusions and believe someone is thinking something bad about us.

  Unknot: Instead of "She thinks I'm useless," remind yourself, "I can't read her mind."

Labelling. I have long hated labels as we can so easily wrongly attribute a label to ourselves or others. With thinking traps, we can add a negative label to ourselves while unknotting the situation. In this way, we attach judgement, shame, and stigma to ourselves.

  Unknot: Instead of "I'm a failure," remind yourself that you made a mistake and do not judge yourself for that mistake.

(continued next page)

Fortune Telling. Self-doubt and a lack of confidence have a lot to answer for when it comes to fortune telling mind traps. We tell ourselves that we will fail before we try.

Unknot: Instead of "This is definitely going to go wrong," remind yourself that no one can predict the future.

Emotional Reasoning. Many of us lean towards listening to our emotions for an answer to life's problems. We attach how we feel onto the situations that occur in our lives meaning when we feel like a rubbish mother, we believe that we are useless, worthless, or pointless.

Unknot: Instead of thinking that our feelings are evidence of our reality, we can accept them and move forward in being objective about what those feelings are conjuring up for us.

Simple Stitches to Unknot Thinking Traps

We can't think our way out of a trap. We can't stop ourselves by saying, "stop thinking that way." That would be all too easy and there is nothing easy about unknotting. Pushing away any upsetting or negative thought means we are not unraveling it, we are not understanding or challenging the thought, so it may very well find its place in our mind once again, tightening that knot. Let's look at some meaningful steps in unknotting our thinking traps.

Separate Your Thoughts

Our thoughts become incredibly knotted and tangled and making sense of them can be a challenge. To begin, we need to separate our thoughts so we can rationalize them. Ask yourself what has happened to lead to this thought? Be as factual as possible at this stage, ensuring that it matches up to the reality of the situation. Then ask yourself, where are you taking the story? What thoughts are cropping up for you and what is your mind telling you about the situation. Identify your emotions, your behaviors, and how you are reacting to the situation. Finally, ask yourself what you are doing to cope or manage the thoughts?

Recognize the Thinking Trap

Once you can separate your thoughts, feelings, and actions, you can look at all your thoughts in their separated glory. Can you recognize any of the thinking traps we have discussed within your thoughts? Are there any distorted thinking patterns popping up?

Challenge the Thinking Trap

Get factual. Remember, our thoughts are often led by our emotions, so it is now time for you to think like a scientist and find the evidence to back up your thoughts. In this way, you are encouraged to challenge your thinking and the possible traps those thoughts have become knotted up with. Ask yourself, what evidence is there to support your thoughts? Would you judge others in the same way you are judging yourself?

When it comes to challenging our thinking, it can be helpful to ask others if they have experienced the same thing. It is one reason why motherhood boards remain so popular. It is a way of bouncing our perceived failures off others and realizing it's not a failure, or a mistake, but perhaps a lesson, growth, or completely natural occurrence when raising babies.

Stitching Up

Simple methods to "unblinker" our thoughts:

- **Recognize the thought.** Instead of ignoring or struggling with a thought, recognize it as being just that, a thought, and not necessarily the reality or truth.
- **Name it.** By naming our blinkered thinking, we acknowledge the thoughts and unknotting them becomes easier. "Ah, this is my knotted thinking again."
- **Make deliberate actions.** We can very easily opt-out when blinkered. Instead, choose to make a deliberate opposing action in order to experience the current thought and feeling.

Stitch 6 ⟶ Psychological Flexibility

And so, we come to psychological flexibility which this book is primarily based on. The ideas, the unraveling, the mindful transition to understanding and loving our motherhood is deeply embedded in our psychological wellbeing and how we respond to the spinning plates of motherhood.

While this final stitch has a section all of its own, and admittedly appears to be the most complex of stitches, know that you are already building on this skill as we have unraveled, chapter by chapter, and repaired, stitch by stitch. Being flexible in our thinking is helped and supported by our acceptance, our self-compassion, our self-care, and recognizing those thinking traps. It encompasses navigating our thought processes to benefit our days.

Let's go back to basics with this final stitch. Parenting, motherhood, transitioning is all so very hard. We are carrying an immense load, attempting to balance homelife and careers, building ourselves up, and raising kids in a wildly fast world. It feels impossible and never-ending at times. How do we navigate the overwhelm, the stress, and the uncertainty of it all? With a little bit of flexibility of course!

Flexible thinking is a difficult challenge because it most often grinds against the way we want to think. Remember, the negativity bias may still have a hold on us, so being flexible in our thinking will challenge the most natural and habitual elements of being human.

However, it also allows and encourages us to remain open and present which in turn helps us:

- To remain engaged with our kids when we are overwhelmed, and the plates are crashing to the floor.
- To rid ourselves of judgements, rigidity in our lives, those open doors, comparisons, and thinking traps.
- To understand ourselves and our children more deeply.
- To lower our stress levels and lean into the calm amid the chaos.
- To connect better with our family and create cohesion throughout our homes.
- To avoid distraction whether it is from our thoughts, feelings, or outside influences.
- To be ok with the discomfort and vulnerable nature of motherhood.
- To understand what kind of mother we would like to be and embracing her.
- To be present and to simply be.

Unknotting

Our thoughts ebb and flow in an unpredictable manner, so it can be difficult to trust our thought patterns. Our flexible thinking includes:

- Holding our thoughts and emotions lightly without clutching them tightly to our chests.

- Recognizing and acting on our long-term goals instead of the instant gratification of short-term actions.

- Accepting rather than resisting the difficult big emotions or knotted thoughts.

- Allowing and accepting our vulnerability, discomfort, and flaws, and then continuing into purposeful action.

Simple Stitches for Psychological Flexibility

Parental psychological flexibility is defined as our ability to accept our negative thoughts, emotions, and beliefs about parenting our children, which allow us to still parent in a way that is effective and beneficial for us and our kids. In essence, with our psychological flexibility we are building on the stitches of mothering ourselves, acceptance, self-compassion, our self-care, and unraveling those thinking traps. We are writing that pattern for ourselves so that we can parent our children in the way that truly reflects our values. So, how can we bend our minds in a way that will support our unraveling, the transition, and our parenting?

Stop Trying to Fix Our Lives and Our Kids

Much of what we do in parenting is about lessons. We teach, but on occasion we can attempt to control. The attempt for control is why I leave my kids clothes or school uniform out for them every morning. It is why I have dictated their behavior when we are in company, or I challenge their choices. As the girls get older, they retaliate and push back. Without being flexible in my thinking, I have pushed back too, and you can imagine how those conversations go—raised voices and slamming of doors. When I resist that urge to be right and maneuver the kids to my way of thinking, I stop. I aim to understand them, rather than control them. It is incredible how when we actively connect with our kids, look them in the eye, listen, and put the phone away, we can see them challenge and advocate for themselves.

Allow for the Vulnerability of Motherhood

I know we have discussed this before, but it is a stitch that needs reinforcing. We will not always get it right and we will often feel exposed and vulnerable in how we unravel and navigate our motherhood. As meaningful as this experience is, it can be incessantly uncomfortable. An extraordinary number of unpleasant and big feelings play out in motherhood—anxiety, stress, irritation, frustration, hurt, and sadness. And that's just on a Tuesday.

Accepting our vulnerability as a mother encourages us to turn towards ourselves with compassion. Remind yourself that it only hurts so much because you care so deeply. Take the moment to pause, to give yourself the space to hold these emotions, and lean into the discomfort by being present and kind to yourself.

Act On Your Values

Our values are the motivating force behind what keeps us going, moving forward, and actively unraveling and stitching up. Remind yourself of the type of person you want to be, about what is important to you in motherhood, about the qualities that are important to you, and what brings you the most joy.

As we become flexible in our understanding of what we want out of our life, we can help guide our kids towards their own values.

Being flexible is not the overall solution to this unraveling but most certainly a stitch we need to unknot. Think of it like mental yoga, helping us to stretch our limits, move our boundaries, and create space to unravel. It is because of this flexibility that we find it easier to unknot, to move in the direction we want, and not be pushed by the thoughts in our minds.

We will move from:

- Feeling stuck in hardship towards coping and managing better.
- Feeling stuck in challenges towards adjusting with the challenges.
- Feeling stuck in fear towards positively navigating that fear.

Stitching Up

Simple methods to build our psychological flexibility:

- Be willing to feel your emotions, including the difficult ones.
- Step back and separate your thoughts.
- Focus on the present.
- Connect rather than compare.
- Live by–and build habits based on–your own values.

A Final Unraveling

HOW DO YOU END a book on a topic that has no ending? I am still unraveling and expect to be until my girls are mothers themselves, if they so choose to be. Even then, I imagine my unraveling will not be over, but take a meaningful shift as mothering never ends.

Stitching up our concept of motherhood is a pattern we work with and amend to suit the outcome we are looking for. We may have unraveled some aspects of our understanding of motherhood over these pages, but there is no guarantee that we have come up with the answers we need just yet. The answers, the understanding, and the truth lies deep within us, how we parent ourselves, trust ourselves, how we are willing to be our own guide, and how well we write the pattern of our motherhood.

No one can write the pattern for us.
I feel this must be emphasized because, in the beginning, as we unraveled cliches, ideologies, and myths, we worked off patterns which were dated, ripped, obscured, and illegible. Patterns we would never wear. This book is largely based off my own pattern, my own understanding (or lack thereof) of motherhood. As a result, there may be elements, conversations, and ideas here which won't relate to your experience.

Motherhood is a lived experience.
Your lived experience. Only you will truly know what needs detangling in your life and how you can stitch up those aspects you are ready to knit. Only you will know and understand the conflicting nature of motherhood in your own life.

Motherhood is conflicting.
It is the conflict between wanting time alone and feeling incredibly lonely. It is the sense that the days are endless, yet they disappear so quickly. It is having those heart-breaking moments but falling with laughter and joy in the next minute. It is everything being so beautiful and perfect yet messy and upended. It is exhaustion and motivation swaddled warmly together. It is rewarding but thankless, natural but confusing, challenging but fulfilling. It is all encompassing yet doesn't define us. It is so very knotted and stitched up at the same time.

Thank you for unraveling with me, for pulling on those threads, finding those knots, and indulging me with that great big metaphor of stitching up. Remember, always remember, the pattern is yours, and if you need support in stitching any of that up, please do ask for help.

Throughout my unraveling I have repeated a mantra to myself which has served me well. As we stitch our final piece of thread together, I will leave you with these words:

I will release the guilt; I will offset the mental load;

I will forgive the forgivable; I will allow the sadness;

I will annihilate the anxiety; I will wander with the daydreams;

I will tune out the loudness; I will cherish the moments;

I will rest my mind.

Acknowledgements

THERE IS SOMETHING WONDERFUL about being given an opportunity to speak so honestly with an audience. But I won't lie, this was not an easy book to write. The rawness of being so open can leave you aching a little as memories bury their way into your headspace, but Barry was there every step of the way. Thank you for holding the spool of my unraveling, for the endless cups of tea, biscuits, Charleston Chew, hugs, understanding, and conversations as these pages were written. Thank you for always being you and going with the flow when I have a "project" on the go. I think we can both agree that this has been my most momentous "project."

Thank you to our girls, Allegra and Devin for being excited for the sun to come up and the cuddles every single morning before we start our day. I am so proud of the people you are. You exhaust me and entertain me in equal measure. I unraveled for you, for me, for us.

Thank you to Andrew Flach and Ryan Tumambing of Hatherleigh Press for taking a chance on a relatively unknown Irish writer with so many thoughts in her head and so many questions to ask—all of which you happily answered for me. You not only guided and supported me in bringing this book to fruition but also understood and shared my vision in creating something that mothers and parents will find powerful, explorative, and metamorphic. Thank you to everyone at Hatherleigh who have pulled this book together. I know it takes a massive group effort.

Special thanks to my editors Ryan Kennedy and Hannah Renouard who understood that my perfectionist tendencies will always find a typo, grammar mistake, or a sentence that would benefit from being rephrased four or five times!

A huge thank you to the incredible contributors who lent their expertise to *Unraveling Motherhood*. Without them, it would have been 250 odd pages of knots and very little stitching up. And that would have been a very different book!

Dr. Malie Coyne, thank you for your beautiful foreword, for knowing how much this book means to me and for always being encouraging when imposter syndrome kicked in. You are an incredibly dynamic woman who has taught me so much about finding the right balance on life, about choosing for ourselves, unraveling, and stitching up.

Dr. Janina Scarlet, if ever there was someone who could tap into my mind without ever meeting me, it's you. You have revolutionized so many people's lives with *Superhero Therapy*, and I hold my hand up as one of those people. Thank you for colliding the world of the nerd with deeply understanding ourselves, and for sharing your wisdom in *Unraveling Motherhood*.

Allison Keating, thank you for being so supportive of this entire process and understanding the rawness and honesty behind my words. You are my daily reminder to nurture every aspect of my life. Your empathy and kindness to all is far reaching, and I am honored you shared that compassion with my readers.

Dr. Mary O'Kane, you wonderful human being. I am forever lightened in your presence, as though you take the knots and tease them out of me as we walk and talk. I am so honored and happy to call you a friend. Always be you. You make the world smile. Thank you for encouraging us all to recognize our own version of perfectly imperfect.

Aisling Leonard-Curtin, your vibrancy and intellect ignites so much in so many of us. I first learned of Acceptance and Commitment Therapy

(ACT) through your passion in breaking down its elements and helping us navigate our lives with ACT. You embraced my willingness to learn, took me under your wing, and opened my mind to a world full of your knowledge and for that I am forever grateful. Thank you being not only a part of this book but of my life.

Dr. Lisa Coyne, thank you for the joy. Parenting is hard, but you show us how our compassionate selves can help us embrace this journey and make it lighter, that boundaries are not only ok but essential. I am grateful you have shared your kindness within these pages.

To my family. My mum and dad, Frances and Oliver Monks, who have always known I'd write a book but most likely didn't expect it to be a non-fiction based on motherhood and psychology. Thank you for recognizing my ailing mental health, for encouraging my recovery, and saying "go for it" when I talked about quitting that librarian job. For always loving me, having my back, and encouraging me. Lorna McCormack, my sister and best friend. Thank you for the countless chats, rants, rages, and tirades about motherhood, life, working from home and for yourself. Our Friday coffee chats are my favorite part of the week. I am lucky to have you in my life. And to Ciarán Monks. Despite living on opposite ends of the earth, if we have learnt anything, it's that miles are meaningless when connection is right there. Thank you for your encouragement and support, for following my career at a distance, and for being my proud big brother.

Avril Flynn, my kindred spirit. You get me; boy, do you get me. Thank you for always being my cheerleader, for knowing what to say, and keeping me grounded. I admire and respect you so much. We have both had one hell of a time unraveling but together we know that knots loosen. Thank you for being by my side.

Eilish Balfe, you are some woman for one woman. A powerhouse with a gentle vulnerability that makes you real and honest and someone to aspire to. I was honored to share this book with you in its very raw stages, even more so when I witnessed you put aspects of *Unraveling Motherhood* into practice. Your texts, words of encouragement, and chats spurred me on. Thank you for being you - a determined, strong, and compelling person.

Triona Gunning, an absolute trailblazer. To say I admire you is an absolute understatement. Thank you for reading those early drafts and helping me make sense of my thoughts, for giving perfect in-depth notes that helped shape my understanding of this book, and for getting it, for simply knowing what I was trying to do. You are a true friend, and I am so thankful that I met you.

Angie Rodrigué, a sincere and special thanks to you for all of the conversations we have had on motherhood over the years. We have always been on the same page, reading from the same book, and exploring all of the themes of what it means to be a woman and a mother in this world. You have helped me unknot more than you will ever know.

Thank you to Paula Flynn without whom I literally would not have had the time to write a word. You have been the official childminder since Allegra was five months old, so why stop when a book needs to be written! Thank you for loving and caring for our girls and giving me the uninterrupted space to write.

To Fiona Forman, Joanna Fortune, Anne M. O'Byrne, Jen Hogan, Ger Callaghan, Helena Tubridy, Beth Kilkenny, Susi Lodola, Maria Rushe, Chris Atkinson, and Sarah Ryan. Thank you all for your support, friendship, and honesty. I could write the book on how important all of you are to me and how you have positively affected my life.

Thank you to Damian Cullen, my editor in *The Irish Times*, who has known about this book for longer than most and has encouraged me to stick it out. It was a goal of mine to write for *The Irish Times* since my dad would come home from work with the paper rolled up under his arm when I was a kid. As a freelancer, the fear is immeasurable when it comes to pitching editors. Will they bite? Have I explained my pitch right? Who am I to write this? With Damian, I feel my contribution to *The Irish Times* is worthwhile, important, and timely. Thank you for giving this writer a shot all those years ago.

Equally, thank you to Roberta von Meding, editor of *Mums & Tots* magazine who was the first editor to commission an article from me. Writing for you is one of those guilty pleasures. You take my ideas, which are usually a little outside of the box, and give me free reign to create something that will empower and support parents. The trust you afford me is the exact encouragement I need as a writer.

Thank you to every editor who saw potential in my writing and yet didn't bite but was willing to read more pitches from me. To every agent and publisher who turned me down because my idea didn't fit their portfolio but encouraged me to keep submitting; for telling me that while their door was closed, there was an open door somewhere because our stories are important.

To every parent I have crossed paths with on social media, especially on Instagram, my preferred space, this book is undoubtedly for you. The understanding, acceptance, and unraveling we have done together, especially in DMs, made those early years of motherhood less lonely, daunting, and expansive. I hope, as you have eased my path, that I have also eased yours.

References

Introduction

1. The Rotunda Hospital Clinical Report, 1st January to 21st December 2013. PDF accessed 04/03/2021 Clinical Rep (rotunda.ie)

2. The Rotunda Hospital Clinical Report, 1st January to 21st December 2017. PDF accessed 04/03/2021 Rotunda Annual Report 2017.pdf

3. Nell Frizzell, (2021) The Panic Years, London: Transworld Publishers Ltd

Chapter 1:
Unraveling Clichés

1. Lamar, M., et al., (2019) Helping Working Mothers Face the Challenges of an Intensive Mothering Culture. *Journal of Mental Health Counselling,* vol 41 (3), pp. 203–220

2. Uriko, K., (2019) Dialogical Self and the Changing Body During the Transition to Motherhood. *Journal of Constructivist Psychology,* vol 32 (3), pp. 221–35

3. Johnston, D. and Swanson, D., (2003) Invisible Mothers: a content analysis of motherhood ideologies and myths in magazines, *Sex Roles,* vol 49 (1/2), pp. 21 -33

4. Woolhouse, M., et al., (2019) "Growing Your Own Herbs" and "Cooking from Scratch": Contemporary discourses around good mothering, food, and class-related identities. *Journal of Community & Applied Social Psychology,* vol 29 (4), pp. 285–296

5. Lamar, M., et al., (2019) Helping Working Mothers Face the Challenges of an Intensive Mothering Culture. *Journal of Mental Health Counselling,* vol 41 (3), pp. 203–220

6. Johnston, D. and Swanson, D., (2003) Invisible Mothers: a content analysis of motherhood ideologies and myths in magazines, *Sex Roles,* vol 49 (1/2), pp. 21 -33

7. Palsson, P., et al., (2018) "I didn't know what to ask about": First time mothers' conceptions of prenatal preparation for the early parenthood period. *The Journal of Perinatal Education,* vol 27 (3), pp. 163–174

8. Clement-Carbonell, C., et al., (2021) Sleep Quality, Mental and Physical Health: A Differential Relationship. *International Journal of Environmental Research and Public Health,* vol 18 (2), pp. 1–8

Chapter 2:
Unraveling Identity

1. Ashforth, B. E., (2001) Role transitions in organizational life: an identity based perspective. Mahwah, NJ: Erlbaum

2. Alvessin, M., & Willmott, H., (2002) Identity regulation as organizational control: producing the appropriate individual. *Journal of Management Studies,* vol 39 (5), pp. 619–644

3. Arnold-Baker, C., (2019) The process of becoming: maternal identity in the transition to motherhood. *Existential Analysis,* vol 30 (2), pp. 260–274

4. Ibid.

5. Laney, E. K., et al., (2013) Expanding the self: motherhood and identity development in faculty women. *Journal of Family Issues,* vol 35 (9), pp. 1227–1251

6. Fyans, P., (2021) *The Invisible Job: how sharing home and parental responsibilities leads to happier lives.* Orpen Press.

7. Scarlet, J., (2020) Super-Women: Superhero Therapy for Women Battling Anxiety, Depression and Trauma. London: Robinson.

Chapter 3:
Unraveling Triggers

1. National Institute for Health and Care Excellence (2014) Mental health in pregnancy and the year after giving birth. https://www.nice.org.uk/guidance/cg192/resources/mental-health-in-pregnancy-and-the-year-after-giving-birth-pdf-250640652229

2. Ou, C. H., & Hall, W. A., (2018) Anger in the context of postnatal depression: an integrative review. Birth: Issues in Perinatal Care, vol 45 (4), pp. 336–346

3. ICD-11: International Classification of Diseases 11th Revision: The global standard for diagnostic health information ICD-11 (who.int)

Chapter 4:
Unraveling Flaws

1. Woodhouse S.S., et al., (2020) Secure Base Provision: A New Approach to Examining Links Between Maternal Caregiving and Infant Attachment. *Child Development,* vol 91 (1), pp. e249—e265

2. Winnicott, D.W. (1971). *Playing and Reality.* London: Tavistock Publications.

3. Twenge, J. M. (2017). *iGen: Why today's super-connected kids are growing up less rebellious, more tolerant, less happy—and completely unprepared for adulthood (and what this means for the rest of us.* New York, NY: Atria Books.

4. Gray P., (2011) *The decline of play and the rise of psychopathology in children and adolescents. American Journal of Play,* vol 3, pp. 443–463

Chapter 5:
Unraveling Control

1. Zhang, Y., et al., (2020) Helicopter Parenting, Parental Psychological and Behavioral Control Revisited. Journal of Comparative Family Studies, vol 51 (1), pp. 59–93

2. Bacikova-Sleskova M, et al., (2021) Parental behavioural control and knowledge in early adolescence. A person-oriented approach. *Current Psychology,* vol 40 (6), pp. 2735–274

3. Leotti, L. A., et al., (2010) Born to choose: the origins and value of the need for control. Trends in Cognitive Sciences, vol 14 (10), pp. 457–463

4. Walsh, G., 2018. *The bald truth about why I shaved my head.* Online Irish Examiner. Available at: https://www.irishexaminer. com/lifestyle/arid-30835590.html

5. Pagnini, F., et al., (2016) Perceived Control and Mindfulness: Implications for Clinical Practice. *Journal of Psychotherapy Integration,* vol. 26 (2), pp. 91–102

6. Rotter JB., (1954) General principles for a social learning framework of personality study. In: J. B. Rotter, ed., *Social Learning and Clinical Psychology.* Prentice-Hall, Inc., pp. 82–104

7. Hovenkamp-Hermelink, J. H. M., et al., (2019) Differential associations of locus of control with anxiety, depression and life-events: A five-wave, nine-year study to test stability and change. *Journal of Affective Disorders,* vol 253, pp. 26–34

8. Nowicki, S., et al., (2021). Editorial: Locus of Control: Antecedents, Consequences and Interventions Using Rotter's Definition. *Frontiers in psychology,* vol 12, 698917

9. Yarritu I., et al., (2014) Illusion of control: the role of personal involvement. *Experimental Psychology,* vol 61 (1), pp. 38–47

10. Leonard-Curtin, A., & Leonard-Curtin, T., (2019) The Power of Small: making tiny but powerful changes when everything feels too much. Dublin: Hatchette Books Ireland

Chapter 6:
Unraveling Boundaries

1. Lindley, J. K., (2020) Know Your Limits. Health, vol 34 (7), pp. 82–85